THE
TWO FACES
OF
CIVIL SOCIETY

THE
TWO FACES
OF
CIVIL SOCIETY

NGOs and Politics
in Africa

Stephen N. Ndegwa

Kumarian Press

mjmayer@Lycos.com, MJM@trywAve.com

The Two Faces of Civil Society: NGOs and Politics in Africa.

Published 1996 in the United States of America by Kumarian Press, Inc., 14 Oakwood Avenue, West Hartford, Connecticut 06119-2127 USA.

Parts of chapter 2 appeared previously in the *International Journal of Comparative Sociology.* Permission to reprint this material is gratefully acknowledged.

Production supervised by Jenna Dixon
Copyedited by Linda Lotz   Proofread by Beth Richards
Index prepared by Barbara DeGennaro

Printed in the United States of America on recycled acid-free paper by Thomson-Shore, Inc. Text printed with soy-based ink.

Library of Congress Cataloging-in-Publication Data
Ndegwa, Stephen N.
    The two faces of civil society : NGOs and politics in Africa / Stephen N. Ndegwa.
        p.   cm. — (Kumarian Press books on international development)
    Includes bibliographical references and index.
    ISBN 1-56549-056-8 (cloth : alk. paper) — ISBN 1-56549-055-X (paper : alk. paper)
    1. Civil society—Africa. 2. Democracy—Africa. 3. Africa—Politics and government—1960–   4. Non-governmental organizations—Africa. 5. Kenya—Politics and government—1978–   6. Non-governmental organizations—Kenya.
I. Title. II. Series.
JQ1879.A15N33   1996
361.7'6'096762—dc20   95-38747

05 04 03 02 01 00 99 98 97 96   10 9 8 7 6 5 4 3 2 1   1st Printing 1996

2000

To Auntie Ann Wanjiru
in memory

Contents

Acknowledgments

I am grateful to many individuals and institutions for providing the support that made the research for this book possible. The Rockefeller Foundation and the Midwest Universities Consortium for International Activities (MUCIA) provided dissertation grants for field research in Kenya between August 1992 and August 1993. MUCIA and the Indiana Center for Global Change and World Peace also provided additional funding for follow-up work in Kenya and Zimbabwe in December 1993. Support from the African Studies Program at Indiana University, Bloomington, enabled me to complete my dissertation and begin revisions toward this book. For this, I am particularly grateful to director Brian Winchester and the staff, who made great colleagues.

Affiliation with the Institute for Development Studies (IDS) at the University of Nairobi during my fieldwork placed me among a stimulating community of scholars from whom I benefited much. I am particularly indebted to H. Karuti Kanyinga and Mutahi Ngunyi for guidance at various stages and to Patrick Alila and Kabiru Kinyanjui for their continued interest in my work. Most importantly, I am indebted to numerous individuals in the NGO sector in Kenya for their willingness to share information and especially to Wangari Maathai of the Green Belt Movement and Ezra Mbogori of the Undugu Society of Kenya for providing unhindered access to these NGOs.

Among friends who cheerfully endured early drafts were Jeff Pickering, Paul Kaiser, and Bruce Heilman. Above all, five people deserve special mention. By their guidance and criticism, C. R. D. Halisi, Patrick O'Meara, York Bradshaw, Russell Hanson, and Freddy Diamant forced me to improve many of my ideas. I can only hope that this book meets the high standards that this company consistently demanded.

Abbreviations
and Glossary

ASDAG	African NGOs Self-Reliance and Development Advocacy Group
CARE	Cooperative for American Relief Everywhere, Inc.
CIDA	Canadian International Development Agency
COTU	Central Organization of Trade Unions
DDC	district development committee
FEMNET	Feminist Network
FORD	Forum for the Restoration of Democracy
GBM	Green Belt Movement
GEMA	Gikuyu Embu Meru Association
IDS	Institute for Development Studies, University of Nairobi
KANU	Kenya African National Union
KENGO	Kenya Energy and Environment NGO
KNCSS	Kenya National Council of Social Services
KPP	Kitui-Pumwani Program
MGG	Middle Ground Group
NANGOF	Namibia NGO Forum
NCCK	National Council of Churches of Kenya
NCWK	National Council of Women of Kenya
NGO	nongovernmental organization
NGOSC	Nongovernmental Organizations' Standing Committee
NORAD	Royal Norwegian Embassy Development Cooperation
NOVIB	Netherlands Organization for International Development Cooperation
OECD	Organization for Economic Cooperation and Development
ORAP	Organization of Rural Associations for Progress
OXFAM	Oxford Committee for Famine Relief
PAGBM	Pan-African Green Belt Movement
PVO	private voluntary organization
SINA	Settlements Information Network Africa

UBEP   Undugu Basic Education Program
UNDP   United Nations Development Program
UNEP   United Nations Environmental Program
UNICEF   United Nations Children's Fund
USAID   United States Agency for International Development
USK   Undugu Society of Kenya
WEDO   Women's Environment and Development Organization

Harambee / literally "pull together" or self-help effort
Kituo cha Sheria / legal aid center
Maendeleo ya Wanawake / literally "development of women";
    national women's organization
Mwakenya / acronym for "solidarity to liberate Kenya"
Nyayo / literally "footsteps"; motto of President Moi's successor
    regime
Undugu / "solidarity" or "brotherhood"

1

The Promise
of Democracy

THIS BOOK EXAMINES how nongovernmental organizations
(NGOs), as part of civil society, contribute to democratization in Africa
and what conditions facilitate or inhibit their contributions. Although
much has been written about how civil society organizations, including NGOs, have significantly altered state-society relations in Africa
over the last decade, we understand little about how this process
unfolds, its determinants, and its limits. Based on comparative case
studies of local NGOs in Kenya, I argue that for NGOs and other organizations in civil society to advance democratization (for instance,
through successful opposition to state control of civic activities), four
conditions must obtain: organization, resources, alliances, and political opportunity. However, as will be evident in the case studies presented, these conditions are not sufficient, especially at the level of
individual NGOs, where a discrepancy emerges between the actions of
two similar NGOs placed in similar circumstances: one actively advo-
cating political pluralism, and the other remaining politically obtuse.

This evidence of the "two faces" of civil society strikes at the heart
of the thesis that civil society organizations such as NGOs necessarily
invest their resources in support of democratization efforts. Even more
troubling, I suggest, is that an important determinant of whether a
well-endowed NGO is transformed into an activist organization is
whether the organization's leadership—often very personalized—
chooses to commit its resources to a progressive political agenda.
Indeed, of the two NGOs studied, it is the more institutionalized one
that when faced with clear opportunities to engage the state in ways
that would advance the democratic ferment in Kenya remains aloof,
even as its own grassroots clients agitate independently. The two faces
of civil society revealed in this book and the centrality of "personal
rule"[1] to political agitation in civil society suggest the need to reexamine present assumptions about the real and potential contributions of

1

organizations in civil society to democratization in Africa. However, as later chapters will show, regardless of the organizational involvement of an NGO in transitional politics, a clear effect of NGO grassroots development work is to enable local communities to independently engage in political actions, with important implications for democratization. For this reason, NGOs remain important, if problematic, contributors to the spread of democracy in Africa.

This study of NGOs and politics in Kenya at the critical juncture of transition from a single-party state to a multiparty democracy provides an opportunity to reexamine the contributions of NGOs and of civil society (broadly) to the process of democratization in Africa. Two issues are important. The first can be summed up as the "civil society–political liberalization" thesis, which is essentially that organizations in civil society, including NGOs, are central to opposing undemocratic governments and to furthering and consolidating democracy. This assumption, as the argument sketched above and as the empirical studies will further elaborate, is problematic at best. The case studies impel a second issue: how to reconceptualize "civil society" in the context of political change in Africa. In particular, what is it about certain organizations in civil society that makes them crucial contributors to democratization?

Civil Society and Political Liberalization

The impetus for the late democratic transitions in Africa has been traced to the growth and political activity of civil society across the continent. Larry Diamond offered perhaps the clearest statement of the rising preeminence of civil society in Africa in fostering political democracy: civil society "has become the cutting edge of the effort to build a viable democratic order" (Diamond, Linz, and Lipset 1988, 26). In recent times, among the most vocal opponents of authoritarian regimes in African countries have been voluntary and associational groups such as the churches, organized labor, professional associations, and grassroots movements (Bratton 1989a; Hyden and Bratton 1992; Chazan 1992). From this mix of civil actors, formidable oppositions have arisen against settled authoritarian regimes: the clergy have riled against incumbent governments; lawyers have challenged illegal state actions; some grassroots movements have pursued independent actions in development activities, and others have evolved into oppositional pressure groups and, eventually, full-fledged opposition parties.

This involvement of civil society in what Samuel Huntington (1991) called the "third wave" of democratization is not unique to Africa. Transitions to democratic rule in eastern and southern Europe and in Latin America were propelled by similar mass action through organized labor, underground movements, and the church (O'Donnell, Schmitter, and Whitehead 1986). Underscoring the centrality of civil society institutions in recent transitions to democracy is the political mobilization they have engendered and their continued political engagement in the liberalized polities, for example, through civic education and election and human rights monitoring (Micou and Lindsnaes 1993). Beyond the immediate transitions from authoritarian rule, many observers view the survival and consolidation of new democracies as similarly predicated on a civil society that is active in delimiting state dominance (Chazan 1992; Harbeson 1994; Bratton 1994; cf. Callaghy 1994; Gyimah-Boadi 1994).

In the following chapters, I examine this promise of civil society as it is exemplified by NGOs in Kenya. I emphasize two particular pitfalls. One is the notion that generic civil society is uniformly progressive in challenging the African state and in advancing democratization. I question the basis of this promise: is it founded on inherent democratic values within civil society, on societal organization and grassroots representation, or on civil society's reaction to external impetuses? The second pitfall is the absence of a notion of grassroots empowerment, which is a result of a singular focus on the organizational or institutional actions of elements of civil society vis-à-vis the state. The relevant question here is, can citizens be empowered to act on their own, rather than having benevolent civil society organizations interceding on their behalf?

In what eventually leads to a nuanced understanding of how NGOs contribute to political change in Kenya, I look at the actions of the collective NGO community in Kenya as it opposed controlling legislation introduced by the government in 1990 (Chapter 3). Many adherents of the civil society–political liberalization thesis would applaud this case as clearly indicating the significance of organizational action in challenging the repressive state in Africa. This case reveals that collective organizational actions by NGOs are indeed important components of the current pressure for political reform in African countries. This case is important less for confirming that NGOs can be democracy-enhancing institutions and more for offering clear indications of the determinants of such actions. Still more significant are the less laudatory aspects that emerge: This case reveals NGOs' dependence on external facilitators for their political actions, especially on international aid donors that provide resources and support and enhance political opportunity. It also reveals that such organizational action to oppose the state at the national level is not accompanied by any complementary action at the grassroot level. Therefore, although this case illustrates NGOs' potential in altering state-society relations, the determinant factors suggest the unlikelihood of such democratizing actions persisting or enduring.

If the actions of the aggregated civil society (the national NGO community) are promising but flawed, those of civil society disaggregated into individual organizations (individual NGOs) are more perplexing. The two NGOs I examine (Chapters 4 and 5) clearly reveal the two faces of civil society: one NGO actively opposes the state and seems to further the democratization movement; the other seeks accommodation to the repressive state, even as opportunities to oppose it arise and, indeed, even as its own clients independently mount opposition to the state. This clearly suggests that civil society's organizational actions are not necessarily oppositional to the state, nor are they democratizing. However, also clearly evident in both cases is the possibility of empowering grassroots communities through an NGO's more mundane activities. In both cases, political activities undertaken by grassroots NGO members or clients suggest more durable contributions to democratization in the presence or absence of institutional actions by the NGO against the state.

In an effort to explain the differences between the two NGOs and why their organizational reactions to the oppositional movement have varied, I uncover a disturbing contradiction to an already nuanced reality of civil society's contributions to democratization. This has to do with the extent to which personal politics permeates the actions of NGOs and of other groups that have been important agitators for political reform in Kenya. For instance, in the Green Belt Movement, the more overtly political of the two organizations examined, challenging actions are personally spearheaded by its leader, Wangari Maathai. In contrast, despite the personal leadership provided to the collective NGO community by the director of the Undugu Society of Kenya in challenging the government on the issue of NGO legislation, that NGO does not openly challenge the Kenyan state. The explanation I offer for this contradiction is that Undugu's institutionalization has mitigated radical political action by its leaders.

The converse of institutionalized leadership in this context is benevolent personal rule akin to the personality politics present in virtually all the groups at the forefront of the movement to force political reform in Kenya, including opposition pressure groups and later parties, the church, and professional associations. These groups have only recently emerged as overt political challengers to the state. As such, their political roles have not been institutionalized, nor have their existing institutional structures been wholesomely open to internal competitive politics. Instead, overt political actions can be traced to a few identifiable individuals in these organizations. Organizational action is therefore strongly correlated with the preferences and actions of individual leaders. This raises an important question: are civil society organizations essentially the resourceful platforms of a displaced elite who are not immune to entrenched interests (such as class or ethnicity)?

As one observer of civil society in Africa noted, being in civil society is the alternative to employment in the civil service.[2] This statement expresses both the possibility and the likely contradiction that civil society may hold for democratic development in Africa. In the 1960s, scholars and development practitioners believed that the African state was the only institution capable of developing newly independent countries (see Huntington 1968). As a result of these expectations, the educated elite joined the civil service, taking it as the arena for directing social, economic, and political change. Development aid from foreign governments followed a similar logic, leading to overflows of bilateral and other aid to the state. But today, the civil service and the state in general have become liabilities to African development and democracy. The current situation presents a reversal of sorts. Development aid is increasingly channeled through nonstate actors (see Chapter 2), and progressive elites for social, economic, and political change are situated in civil society. Will civil society act any differently from the civil service (the state) to deliver on the promise of democracy?

The diversity among NGOs' positioning with regard to the democratization movement suggests that the blanket civil society–political liberalization thesis requires revision. The revised thesis need not deny the importance of civil society actors in the recent political transformations—it would be foolhardy to argue against the evidence (see Hyden and Bratton 1992). Instead, the revised thesis should address a different set of questions: Which actors in civil society are important to the transition to democracy? Which actors will be important to the consolidation of democracy? And, more fundamentally, why are some actors in civil society actively involved in the democratic movement, whereas others remain oblivious, take the free ride, or are actually hostile?

Reconceptualizing Civil Society and Democratic Change

The empirical studies that follow prompt a reconsideration of what it is about civil society organizations that make them supportive of democratization efforts.[3] In this regard, I suggest that there is nothing inherent about civil society organizations that makes them opponents of authoritarianism and proponents of democracy. Rather, the impetus for civil society's involvement in the democratization movement can be located in two externalities: a wider social movement and political opportunity.

According to Charles Tilly (1978), social movements refer to three converging components: "to the actors (groups) involved; to the values, beliefs, and claims (issues) articulated; and to the actions (events) carried out" (Kriesi 1988, 350). Like any other social movement, the democratic movement can be expressed in organized civil society or diffused in unorganized society. The recent protests against repressive governments in Africa represent such social movements—the convergence of different *actors* (civil society, donors, political parties) articulating democratic *values* (human rights, freedom of speech) and pursuing *actions* (demonstrations, boycotts) to challenge authoritarian regimes. Although such a social movement may be expressed in or by some parts of civil society, it is not synonymous with the generic civil society. Civil society constituents such as local voluntary organizations or associational bodies can be said to contribute to the democratic ferment in Africa only if they embrace and express this social movement.

Combining the notion of civil society with that of social movements has recognizable advantages in examining democratic transitions in Africa. A social movement implies a dynamic in a given direction and a core set of overriding values that binds different actors to the same broader goal. Within the present context, a social movement may be progressive (democratic) or reactionary (antidemocratic); its core values are shared by actors (churches, lawyers, organized labor, and so forth) whose primary organizational interests may differ radically. The same cannot be said about civil society, which, by definition, implies diverse, narrow interests not necessarily joined together but sharing the "space" outside the state. The only ideology that civil society celebrates in common is the pluralism that allows individual groups to exist, advocate, and pursue their goals—including some that may undermine this very pluralism. The notion of a social movement that an organization may choose to embrace or oppose allows us to understand why some civil society organizations may not act in ways that are supportive of democratic change.

In terms of democratic transitions in Africa, it is therefore more prudent to argue that for organizations in civil society to be supportive of democratization, they have to embrace this social movement: that is, articulate democratic values as well as pursue actions to challenge nondemocratic regimes. That not all civil society actors are so disposed is evident from the NGOs examined in later chapters. More broadly, in several cases in Africa, where the formerly repressive state allowed a greater expansion of civil society actors and activities, antidemocratic forces were also unleashed in various hues *in* civil society. Examples include the fundamentalist Islamic parties in Algeria, the township violence in South Africa, and the interethnic violence in Kenya. Civil society cannot therefore be assumed to be congenial to or supportive of democratic pluralism by its mere existence, expansion, or level of activity (Bayart 1986, 118; Bratton 1989a, 430; Callaghy 1994; Gyimah-Boadi 1994). It must be expressive of the social movement or consciousness for establishing, practicing, and preserving democratic values and institutions. In focusing on the role of civil society in democratic transitions and consolidation in Africa, it is imperative that analysts look to those organizations that express this dynamic rather than to generic civil society.

A second factor that explains the overwhelming success of civil society in forcing political concessions in Africa relates to the availability of opportunity to mobilize, agitate, and bargain with the state from a position of strength. I contend that recent successes achieved by organizations in civil society are far from an automatic outgrowth of previous political challenges, many of which were crushed outright by the state. Instead, they are a result of unique circumstances amounting to what some have referred to as "protest season," "cycles of protest," or "political opportunity" (Tarrow 1991).

Sidney Tarrow suggests that protest movements "tend to cluster in distinct historical periods" that are characterized by "an expanding structure of political opportunities" (1991, 13). Tarrow cites empirical studies that buttress this point (1991, 14): for example, on American protests that appeared (and seemed to thrive) in a few recognizable crisis periods, such as during critical elections (see Goldstone 1980); on urban protest movements in Latin American cities that were associated with available political openings (see Leeds and Leeds 1976); and on prolonged protests in post–World War II Italy that were influenced by the dealignment and realignment of Italian party politics in the 1960s and 1970s (see Tarrow 1989). The continent-wide mobilization of Africa's peoples against colonization in the post–World War II years represents events whose origins have yet to be explored in this light. Tarrow suggests that the expansion of "political opportunity" precedes a wave of mobilization in which organized publics challenge the status quo because the risks of such action are lower and the likelihood of success higher during such openings in the political system (1991, 15).

Prior to the 1990s, civil society organizations in Africa had been subjugated by the state. Although accounts of the independence struggles in many African countries suggest the deep political involvement of societal organizations in the preindependence years, after independence, many of these institutions were either co-opted, suppressed, or outlawed outright by the state (Kasfir 1976). The previous inactivity of social organizations in the political arena (with the exception of those annexed by the ruling single parties) and the academic focus on the state have made the current explosion in the number of organizations and their political activity appear to be novel. The coincidence of this political activity with opposition movements against the single-party state has suggested for many analysts that civil society and democratization are an inseparable twain.

The failures of many oppositional efforts against the single-party state in Africa (especially in the 1970s and early 1980s) suggest the importance of the opportunity for successful protest presented by a period of generalized political mobilization. For instance, protests that occurred when African states were not in a state of crisis (outside a wave of mobilization) were easily crushed or lost momentum due to swift repressive action by authoritarian regimes. In Kenya, one of the groups that sought to challenge President Daniel arap Moi's stranglehold on power was *Mwakenya*—a Swahili acronym for "the solidarity to liberate Kenya." It was a clandestine movement composed of intellectuals, students, and exiled politicians who sought to undermine the single-party regime through underground grassroots mobilization in the early and mid-1980s. However, *Mwakenya* was effectively neutralized through the arrest and conviction of many of its leaders and recruits in Kenya and the exile of its intellectual sympathizers (see Ngunyi and Gathiaka 1993). Unfortunately for the movement, it had appeared just at the height of Moi's successful effort to consolidate state power and the lowest point of political opportunity. In the case of NGOs in Kenya in the 1990s, their propensity to agitate and the concessions they extracted from the state were significantly facilitated by the available political opportunity resulting from a single-party state besieged by grassroots protests, nationwide party-level agitation, and pressure from international donors to reform.

The Kenyan Case in Context

As is the case with other African countries in transition from authoritarian rule, politics in Kenya is presently in a state of flux. The return of the former single-party Kenya African National Union (KANU) to power following the 1992 multiparty elections has lent much uncertainty to the direction of change. Nevertheless, despite a constrained pluralism, there are more possibilities for political mobilization and opportunities for organizations in civil society to influence democratic change. In particular, given the weak and divided opposition parties, progressive organizations such as churches and NGOs involved in development have an opportunity to pursue an empowerment agenda within their sphere of activities. In Kenya, and in other countries under transition, this period presents an opportunity to mobilize civic publics and to influence the direction of political change toward greater participatory democracy and accountable government.

Formerly a single-party state for much of its three decades of independence, Kenya remains one of the more stubborn converts to multiparty politics and to the finer details of political liberalization. In Kenya, as in many other African countries, the common elements thought to have contributed to a shift to multiparty politics are the demonstration effect of the reverberating eastern European democratization, the pressure from donor countries and organizations for political and economic reforms, and the groundswell of national and grassroots agitation within the country. Both international and local NGOs in Kenya have exerted pressure for political reforms at the international, national, and grassroot levels, but most visibly at the former two levels.

Kenya is a particularly attractive case for the study of NGO-state relations, since it has the highest number of both international and local NGOs in sub-Saharan Africa (Bratton 1989b; KNCSS 1987). This is mainly a result of three factors that make it an attractive area or base of operations: Nairobi's status as a regional center for international organizations, complemented by a well-developed communication network; Kenya's relative political stability, which has allowed NGOs to operate openly and widely; and the spirit of *Harambee* (self-help), which has been widely cultivated as a development ideology since independence and has given rise to over 20,000 local self-help groups (Ngethe and Kanyinga 1990). This enormous growth of local self-help groups reveals the great role that nongovernmental and voluntary organizations play in development activities and their legitimacy as a fundamental feature of Kenya's political and civic life—especially as they have become potential or actual clients of political patrons and the state (Holmquist 1984).

The Kenyan government's resistance to political liberalization, coupled with the great number of NGOs and especially the active opposition to the government among some of them, makes Kenya an interesting case to explore. Moreover, the government's ambivalence toward NGOs calls further attention to unresolved tensions between them. This ambivalence is best reflected in the state's embracing NGOs as "partners in development" in its recent development plans (Ngethe, Mitullah, and Ngunyi 1990, 1), yet guarding against their influence as agents of sociopolitical change with a wariness underscored by the speedy passage of the controlling NGO Coordination Act of 1990, which I examine in greater detail in Chapter 3. This dialectic, with its pendulum swings of suspicion and acceptance, cooperation and rebuff, makes Kenya an ideal case for examining NGOs in the context of state-society relations—especially the nuances of democratic renewal contained in them. Given a growing awareness among NGOs in Africa of the need to reevaluate their identity and their role in and relations with African states and the rest of civil society, lessons from the Kenyan experience (which is largely seen as an exemplar by NGOs, especially in eastern and southern Africa) should be of interest to those who work with or study NGOs in Africa.[4]

The Case Studies

In looking at the potential for civil society to influence democratic transitions, I examine NGOs in Kenya at three levels. First, I examine how NGOs as a community exemplify civil society's challenge to the state through their collective agitation against controlling legislation. In particular, I seek to highlight the factors (such as increased resources and collective organization) that facilitate success in such political agitation. Second, I examine NGOs as individual actors and highlight their specific challenges to the state as well as differences between the two NGOs selected. Finally, I examine how the selected NGOs work with grassroots clients to empower them to participate in challenges against the repressive state or in democratic political processes.

In the chapters that follow I present a comparative case study of two local NGOs: the Undugu Society of Kenya and the Green Belt

Movement (GBM). The Undugu Society (*Undugu* is a Swahili word for "brotherhood" or "solidarity") is a development organization whose main focus is improving the lot of the urban poor in Nairobi and its environs. Its concern with the urban poor is a response to the pressures of urbanization in Kenya. In particular, the recent economic recession and the economic liberalization measures that have further impoverished a greater portion of the urban population make such an NGO extremely important to current development and economic recovery efforts in Kenya. The GBM focuses on mobilizing rural women countrywide for environmental conservation through tree planting. The GBM straddles two equally important areas: the role of women in development, especially in the rural areas, and the environment, which can scarcely be divorced from agriculture (Kenya's foremost economic sector)—of which women are the overworked guardians.

These two NGOs represent important organizational actors located at the center of recent pressures for political change in Kenya. Undugu has been involved in the poor urban communities, many of which were ardent supporters of multiparty advocates in 1990–92. The GBM has itself challenged the state on environmental issues arising out of official development programs. It has also spawned a political consciousness for the multitude of underprivileged—in particular, rural women. Both organizations have also been important actors (mainly in the persons of their leaders) in shaping NGO-state relations through either collective bargaining or outright challenges to the overbearing state. Because of their relatively long existence, these two indigenous NGOs are a conspicuous feature and a felt presence in the NGO sector in Kenya and are models for many others in the country. Although there are hundreds of NGOs in Kenya, the GBM and Undugu are the largest and most well-known local (Kenyan), nonreligious NGOs. Smaller NGOs receive hardly any attention from government officials, the news media, or the public, but Undugu and the GBM do.

Both NGOs were formed at about the same time (Undugu in 1975 and GBM in 1977). This situates them in the same historical context and permits a comparison of their actions and reactions to similar sociopolitical contexts. Both have a history of cooperation with government agencies, but, for the GBM, this has changed. There is also a difference in the geographical focus of their activities: the GBM spans Kenya, whereas Undugu concentrates on Nairobi. Finally, Undugu has had a turnover in leadership over the last two decades, and the GBM has maintained the same leadership. This enables a comparison of institutional growth as well as changing goals linked to the leadership.

In examining these cases, I seek to demonstrate the aspects of NGO operations that are important in political mobilization and the possibilities for individual NGOs to influence fundamental political change. My comparative analysis provides insight into how NGO activities affect state-community relations and eventually contribute to the demands for democratic change in Kenya. The process can be encapsulated tentatively as follows: The activities of an NGO influence its target community's political culture by fostering grassroots participation within its universe of activities and sensitizing the community to the causes of its problems, which may involve state neglect or complicity. Within its activities, the NGO instills in its clients a sense of efficacy and empowerment by practicing and encouraging democratic values and self-determination. However, beyond this arena the community encounters a state that remains nonrepresentative, nonparticipatory, and nonresponsive. The state's actions are thus exposed as antithetical to the new community values of participation, and its legitimacy is eroded. The community or individual encountering such contradictions is then more likely to press for its rights or to participate in efforts to transform the state toward a more participatory polity.

If the political impact of NGOs in Kenya can be comprehended, this knowledge can inform future policies pursued by actors interested in fostering democratic change in Africa—in particular, NGOs and donor agencies. The findings presented in the following chapters are generalizable to other NGOs in Kenya and in other countries. Since I focus on the *processes* of NGO engagement with the state and the fostering of political consciousness and empowerment through the mundane cycle of project implementation, it is possible to infer key lessons that are applicable to other democratizing countries. Theoretically, the findings reported here elaborate a critique of current thinking on civil society's capacity to influence the process of democratization in Africa.

Notes

1. According to Jackson and Rosberg (1982, 17–22), "personal rule" refers to a system of governance under which the ruler determines the issues, the rules, and often the outcomes of political relations; this role is neither institutionalized nor purposively constrained by impersonal institutions. Although this model was developed and has been widely applied with regard to the African state, it has not been discussed in relation to organizations in civil society.

2. Personal communication from Louis Helling, Indiana University, 1993.
3. For more comprehensive theoretical discussions of the concept of civil society and its recent application in Africa, see Harbeson, Rothchild, and Chazan 1994; Ekeh 1992.
4. For example, the 1994 "Workshop on an Enabling Environment for NGOs in Eastern and Southern Africa," held in Windhoek, Namibia, was devoted to examining lessons from the Kenyan experience to inform strategies for NGOs in Tanzania, Uganda, Zambia, Zimbabwe, Botswana, Lesotho, and South Africa.

2

The Political Context of NGOs in Africa

OVER THE LAST TWO DECADES, there has been growing evidence of the inability of the African state to deliver on its development promise. Indeed, the state in Africa has variously been described as "weak" or "soft"—in other words, unable to pursue its objectives (Migdal 1988; Jackson and Rosberg 1986). Progressively, the proposition that the postindependence African state is indeed the *problem* and the inhibitor of social, economic, and political development has become the common view among students of African development. This amounts to a turnaround in development theory, which previously held the state to be the ultimate purveyor of development in Africa. That this shift has taken root in the current thinking on development is suggested not only by the expansive literature on the demise of the African state and the ascendancy of civil society (Rothchild and Chazan 1988) but also by the policies of donor agencies and development practitioners (see Brown and Korten 1989; Best and Brown 1990; World Bank 1989).

Thus, in the study of political development, analysts have come full circle from the statist arguments of the late 1960s and 1970s. For example, the previous concern with the ability of newly independent states to govern (and develop) their populations (Huntington 1968) has evolved into the present preoccupation with the legitimacy of states in civil society (Hyden and Bratton 1992). The serious and largely successful challenges faced by formerly autocratic states from their citizens (for example, in eastern Europe and Latin America) have thrust the question of democratization to the fore in the study of political development. The prevailing wisdom holds that to institute governments that are anchored in democratic institutions and ethos such as accountability and transparency (euphemistically referred to as "good governance"), it is necessary to have an active and developed civil society that will hold the state to account in various arenas.

15

Looking at NGOs in Africa as part of civil society, Alan Fowler (1991b) finds them incapable of contributing to democratization. Fowler cites a number of reasons that NGOs are unable to advance the political liberalization agenda in African countries. One is especially important here. He argues that the project financing mode that is the norm with NGOs involved in development work hardly features "emancipatory" issues (for example, land reform or empowering underprivileged groups) but instead focuses on "modernization" projects such as small business credit, shelter for the poor, and family planning (70). This leads to a situation in which donors finance NGOs "for what they do—implement projects—rather than what they can be—politically pluralizing entities" (74). Fowler therefore advocates a more deliberate effort by donors to strengthen civil society, especially by supporting advocacy and internal democratization of NGOs via transparency, accountability, and institution building. According to Fowler, the democratization effect of NGOs must be deliberately sought and not expected to automatically spin off from NGO modernization projects.

Despite his well-founded suspicions, Fowler shares with other observers the view that NGOs could pluralize civil society in Africa and thus contribute to democratization. Bratton (1989a, 412) further affirms that as the state withdraws from its myriad functions, "groups within civil society will enjoy greater opportunities to attract a following, *develop a bureaucratic form,* and formulate policy alternatives" (emphasis added). In considering the contributions of NGOs to democratization, these observers view NGOs primarily as *institutions.* This is as it should be, given the broad definition of civil society as an "ensemble of organizations" that relate to the state (Stepan 1988). What most analysts have overlooked, however, is that the pluralizing effects of civil society organizations can democratize only their "space," not that of grassroots communities that remain disempowered. Thus the pluralizing effects of NGOs in civil society may be only half the battle. To fully democratize African societies, NGOs must contribute to the empowerment of grassroots communities.

To emphasize that this is not a hairsplitting exercise, one needs only recall the experience of numerous political groupings (such as tribal or ethnic interest groups or trade unions) at the time of independence in many African countries. At the time, civil society as an organizational arena was well populated and active. However, within the first decade of independence, much of this vibrant civil society had been undermined by the state. The masses had not been empowered, and civil society institutions can be empowered only by their members. Therefore, despite the facade of institutional pluralism (including opposition parties), civil society and pluralism itself were being undermined by the state and state elites. In particular, civil society organizations were dissolved under the ideology of the single party that held multiparty politics and its corollary interest-group pluralism to be detrimental to the nation-building exercise. The result was the "mass-based" single-party state that has recently faced a formidable onslaught from civil society's reassertion of itself. Although "enlarging" and "safeguarding" civil society (Kinyanjui 1989) are crucial to opening avenues for political participation, empowering the masses is the surest way to sustain democracy and development. An organization that does not empower its members (or clients), even though it may pluralize civil society (merely by its own existence), does naught for democratization.

The Growth of the NGO Sector in Development

Although the existence of private voluntary organizations can be traced as far back as the turn of this century, their sustained involvement in relief and development work, first in the North and eventually in the developing world, is essentially a post–World War II phenomenon (Fowler 1988; Helmich 1990). Most of the large NGOs were formed in the wake of the two world wars for the purpose of contributing to the reconstruction of war-ravaged Europe. Thus, the American relief NGO, Cooperative for American Relief Everywhere (CARE) was formed in 1945; the Oxford Committee for Famine Relief (OXFAM) was formed in 1948 in Britain (Kanyinga 1993). After Europe's reconstruction and with the advent of political independence for African and Asian countries in the 1950s and 1960s, these organizations shifted to development work in these areas. However, up until the late 1970s and early 1980s, NGOs remained peripheral actors in Third World development, since most of the development aid given at the time was bilateral. However, starting in the early 1980s, the expansion in the NGO sector and its growing involvement in development work across the world were overwhelming (Bratton 1989b; Drabek 1987; Fowler 1988). This growth was also indicative of the emerging realization that the African state was a stumbling block to development because of its lack of accountability. As a result of this expansion, NGO contributions to social and economic development in the developing world have been impressive (Best and Brown 1990; Brown and Korten 1989).

The number of NGOs in the developing world has grown tremendously over the last two decades and is conservatively estimated at between 6,000 and 8,000 (OECD 1990, 24). The number of NGOs in Organization for Economic Cooperation and Development (OECD) countries alone rose from 1,700 in 1981 to 2,000 in 1987 and is currently estimated to be over 2,500 (OECD 1990; Fowler 1988). The expanding role of NGOs in development is evident in the amount of development resources they collectively manage and in the increasing instances of their cooperation with and influence on other bodies involved in development work. The United Nations estimates that NGOs are responsible for the transfer of an estimated US$5 billion in development aid from the North to developing countries (UNICEF 1993). This represents 12.5 percent of the total bilateral transfer of US$40 billion to the developing nations. This is a substantial contribution, since it is equivalent to the total official aid given to developing countries that is devoted to core concerns such as basic needs (UNICEF 1993, 46). The amount of resources that Northern NGOs attract from both official and private sources to transfer to developing countries has also experienced tremendous growth. For instance, contributions by the Canadian International Development Agency (CIDA), which was among the first official aid agencies to provide matching grants to NGOs, reflect this growth (Brodhead 1987). Between 1976 and 1984, CIDA disbursements to NGOs rose from Can$37.6 million to Can$249 million. In percentage terms, this reflects a rise from a paltry 4 percent of CIDA's total disbursements in 1976 to 12 percent of the 1984 total disbursement (Brodhead 1987, 23). Brian Smith (1987, 88) noted that official aid to NGOs from European, Canadian, and North American official aid agencies more than tripled, from US$331.9 million in 1973 to US$1.1 billion in 1985. This trend has continued, especially among OECD member countries, particularly with recent emergency relief operations that NGOs have mounted (Smillie and Helmich 1993).

At the international level, NGOs have become prominent coactors with many intergovernmental and multilateral aid bodies, such as the World Bank and various United Nations agencies involved in relief, environmental, and development work. The World Bank, which is the largest multilateral donor, has come to recognize the important position NGOs occupy in the development process. Starting in the early 1980s, the bank consciously moved from "listening to NGOs to working with them" by initiating efforts toward greater cooperation (Quereshi 1988, 13). As early as 1980, the World Bank had started to explore ways and means of involving NGOs in its projects, which are essentially undertaken by governments. These efforts have resulted in several instances of cooperation between NGOs and the World Bank: for instance, between 1973 and 1979, NGOs were involved in

71 bank projects; between 1980 and 1988, they were involved in another 128 projects (Salmen and Eaves 1989). In 1989 alone, NGOs were involved in close to 50 bank projects (World Bank 1990, 8). More importantly, NGO involvement in bank projects was moving from mere implementation to all stages of the project cycle: identification, design, appraisal and financing, implementation, and evaluation (Salmen and Eaves 1989; see also Engelstad 1989). In recent reports, the World Bank has openly stated its recognition of the role NGOs could play in improving local participation in development and in contributing to "institutional pluralism" to check government policy performance (World Bank 1994, 125). NGOs have similarly been involved in an increasing number of projects with national official aid agencies such as the U.S. Agency for International Development (USAID) (*African Voices,* spring 1994) and even more closely with the United Nations through the UN Nongovernmental Liaison Service (WEDO 1994b, 3) and through agencies such as the United Nations Children's Fund (UNICEF), the United Nations Development Program (UNDP), and the United Nations Environmental Program (UNEP).

Moreover, NGOs have set up their own global, regional, or interest-area networks that command considerable resources and have a considerable voice in development policy matters. These networks are relatively new; they facilitate contact among NGOs as well as with donors and governments and provide a forum for the discussion and coordination of NGO activities (Stremlau 1987). The sheer presence and policy demands of the NGO sector at the 1992 Earth Summit in Brazil, the 1994 Population Summit in Cairo, and the 1995 Women's Conference in Beijing speak to their massive organizational capacity and resources as well as to their voice in global development issues. The global NGO community has also made spirited attempts to press for more supportive economic, social, or diplomatic policies toward the marginalized developing world. For example, since 1984, NGOs have mounted "The Other Economic Summit," a highly visible alternative meeting parallel to and at times a block away from the annual summit of the G-7 (the most industrialized countries) (*Daily Nation,* July 18, 1991).

The global expansion of the NGO sector in development is more clearly reflected at the country level in developing nations. In Kenya, for which fairly complete data are available, the total number of registered NGOs rose from 124 in 1975 to over 400 in 1987; the subset of international NGOs rose from 37 in 1978 to 134 (a 260 percent increase) in 1987, and the number of local, indigenous NGOs rose from 57 to 133 (a 130 percent increase) in the same period (Fowler 1989). A more recent figure put the estimate at a total of 500 NGOs in

Kenya (*Kenya Times,* February 14, 1990). Similarly, other countries are hosts to large numbers of active NGOs: for example, Uganda with 250 (Coninck 1992), Zambia with 128, Tanzania with 130, Zimbabwe with 300 (NGO Task Force 1991), and Namibia with over 55 (NAN-GOF 1992).

The growing role of NGOs is also evident at the country level from the amount of development resources they bring into their host countries. It is estimated that the NGO sector in Kenya has an annual development expenditure of US$150 to 200 million (Lekyo 1989; Fowler 1991b; InterAction 1986; UNDP 1989). A more recent survey estimates that official aid to Kenyan NGOs amounts to about US$35 million a year, which is about 18 percent of all official aid received by Kenya annually; similarly, in Uganda, NGOs disburse an estimated 25 percent of all official aid to Uganda (NGO Task Force 1991). In more concrete terms, the Kenyan government concedes that NGOs provide 30 to 40 percent of Kenya's total development expenditure (Ngethe, Mitullah, and Ngunyi 1990). Often quoted is the fact that NGOs provide more than 40 percent of all health care services in Kenya and, in particular, between 40 and 45 percent of all family planning services (*Daily Nation,* April 19, 1989; Kanyinga 1993). Given the weakening financial capacity of the Kenyan government, these figures may well be on the increase. Indeed, as the government readily admits, the NGO contribution to health care services may rise to 50 percent in the near future (Kanyinga 1993). Similar trends are evident in other sectors of development in Kenya (for example, education and agriculture) and in other countries in Africa, due in part to economic structural adjustment programs.

The expansion of the NGO role in development work has been fueled by a prominent shift in the traditional strategies of development administration. The channeling of immense resources through NGOs reflects the conventional wisdom regarding the ability of official development agencies and, in particular, African states to carry out development work. Riddled by inefficiency, corruption, and authoritarianism and generally lacking in accountability to its citizens, the African state has been isolated as the greatest bottleneck to developing African countries. Northern official aid agencies have also failed to deliver sustainable development because of their reliance on African governments or their own inability to reach the poorest populations (Best and Brown 1990). NGOs, in contrast, have been viewed as efficient, less bureaucratic, grassroots oriented, participatory, and contributing to sustainable development in grassroots communities (Fowler 1991b; Best and Brown 1990; but cf. Mitullah 1990; Tandon 1991). This preference for NGOs reflects a fundamental tenet in current development theory and practice that holds in disdain existing official or state arrangements and seeks to "get government off the backs of the people" by elevating private and public nonstate actors (see especially World Bank 1989; also *Africa Recovery*, December 1993–March 1994, 34).

The decline of the state in Africa has also provided entry points for both foreign and local NGOs to embark on development work—for instance, when states have been unable to provide adequate services such as health care, education, and agricultural and credit extension. In Kenya, as the government's budgetary outlays to both education and health care have fallen, NGOs have entered these fields and become indispensable partners in service provision. Similarly, as Kanyinga (1993) points out, recurrent droughts, famines, and civil strife have provided entry points for essentially humanitarian relief NGOs that have lingered to pursue development work after the initial calamity. The recent Somalia debacle illustrates a situation in which relief NGOs may have to stay on and help reconstitute the social and economic infrastructure and, eventually, facilitate the political one after the end of the war. Furthermore, the implementation of structural adjustment programs has strained the ability of African states to provide services and has attracted more NGOs to cushion the adverse short-term effects of adjustment programs, such as by providing affordable health services (see Clark 1990). Given the present economic and political conditions in Africa, it is likely that the number and role of NGOs engaged in development will expand even more and, with this, their role in the social, economic, and political arenas.

NGO Growth and Growing Political Tensions with States

The growing presence and capacity of NGOs in all sectors of development and their "overtaking" of states in some instances due to the states' decreasing capacity have put the two on a sure collision course. As Fowler (1991b, 57) points out, NGO activities that overshadow the state tend to be viewed as direct challenges to the "imperatives of statehood"—territorial hegemony, security, autonomy, legitimacy, and revenue (see also Young 1988). For most postindependence African states these "imperatives" have been anchored in the state's ability to "deliver development" and are therefore endangered by its eroded capacity to do so or by the presence of alternative suppliers. This is especially true when NGOs spread out to all corners of their host countries in pursuit of their goals, sometimes even to the most remote or most strife-torn regions, where their host governments may not have secured these "imperatives of statehood" (for example, northern Uganda or southern Sudan). For this reason, African governments have come to view NGOs as socioeconomic assets but also more warily as political challengers whose benevolence needs to be directed and coordinated in order not to undermine the state. This attitude does not differ much from the attitude that African states have adopted toward other independent loci of power such as the church, opposition parties, radical intellectuals, ethnic associations, and even traditional monarchies.

Governments in Africa are therefore concerned about the growth and activities of NGOs on two *political* counts: (1) because they constitute a network of resourceful organizations that are growing more autonomous of the state, and (2) because they have the potential to change state-society relations in the grassroots communities they work in (see Bratton 1989b). On their part, NGOs have exacerbated these concerns somewhat unwittingly by challenging the state's position as the sole or prime development agent—especially by penetrating areas that the state has been unable or unwilling to reach. Some NGOs have also taken bold actions to challenge state policies or actions, especially those relating to the administration of development aid and political reforms. Moreover, the decline of official aid to states in Africa and the more recent withdrawal or conditionality of the remainder have not endeared NGOs to states that view them as competitors. The ensuing "political jealousy" has led governments to attempt to control NGOs and their resources in the name of preserving national sovereignty.

In Kenya, the government responded to NGO political challenges by effecting the NGO Coordination Act of 1990, which sought to monitor and control NGO activities. This legislation was a contentious issue and is one of the areas in which NGOs have enabled civil society expansion and empowerment in Kenya. In Uganda, the government introduced similar legislation that placed NGOs under its internal security secretariat in 1989. Prior to that, in 1987, the Ugandan government had banned the use of radios by NGOs for cross-country communication (*Weekly Review,* June 19, 1992). Similarly, the Zimbabwean government shut down operations of the Organization of Rural Associations for Progress (ORAP), which was operating in the troubled Matabeleland region (Bratton 1989b, 579). Other instances of African governments clamping down on NGOs, ostensibly precipitated by challenges to the "imperatives of statehood," can be found in Ethiopia, Sudan, Zambia, Tanzania, and South Africa (Bratton 1989b; *Weekly Review,* June 19, 1992).

Despite these tensions, NGOs have maintained the goal of empowering grassroots communities as a crucial step toward social, economic, and political recovery in Africa. In particular, leading NGOs (especially the larger and older local NGOs) and regional NGO consortia have become more explicit about their goals of empowering their clients. For instance, the African NGOs Self-Reliance and Development Advocacy Group (ASDAG) urges member NGOs to explicitly state their own commitment to "people empowerment" and to suggest how this can be achieved through their development activities. In addition, it urges them to foster grassroots participation and democratic processes in their own internal decision making on projects (ASDAG 1991, 2). However, some NGOs in eastern and southern Africa are well aware of their own limitations with respect to influencing the political process. In a survey, they admitted that:

> NGOs in the region lack influence in the political process and have little macro-level impact. They either do not comprehend or often ignore the larger context in which they operate, focusing only on the micro-level, and most fail to recognize that the communities they serve are part of systems that are strongly influenced by poor internal policies and negative external forces. (NGO Task Force 1991, 5)

Such self-critiques have fueled NGO efforts to break from their "atomized" project activities and pursue greater advocacy work toward altering the life conditions of their grassroots communities. This includes efforts to "exercise greater leadership in addressing the negative aspects of policy and unsatisfactory institutional settings within which they work . . . [and] . . . to challenge the structures of impoverishment that keep their constituencies destitute." Furthermore, they assert, "as professed supporters of the marginalized and the disenfranchised . . . NGOs have the moral mandate and responsibility to channel grassroot perspectives and concerns to policy formulations" (NGO Task Force 1991, 5).

However, NGOs find that their host governments are often unreceptive to this kind of "development." In many instances, governments have instituted control mechanisms to contain such advocacy goals by NGOs. One of the overriding issues for NGOs in Africa has therefore been the need for greater autonomy from the state to choose and to pursue their development objectives (ASDAG 1991; NGO Task Force 1991). Faced by a hostile state that has denied them an "enabling environment," NGOs are evolving a collective will to assert themselves. This is evident in their bold resolution that "NGOs must be prepared to challenge state activities which they find inconsistent with the interests of their constituency, as well as oppose legislation and administrative steps which undermine their autonomy and participation in the development process" (NGO Task Force 1991, 7). NGOs in Africa are keenly aware of their "pluralizing" role in civil society and of the need to organize collectively, be assertive (Bratton 1989a), and seek their own and their clients' empowerment (Fowler 1991b).

Once again, it is important to point out that most of the strategies and limitations that NGOs consider in their "political" work relate to them as *institutions* through which grassroots communities can channel their interests. As such, NGOs become intermediary organizations, much like other interest groups in civil society. This is the broad understanding that NGOs (along with students of NGOs and civil society) have embraced about their role in democratization. The implication here is that NGOs are important contributors to democratization to the extent that they become actors in "freeing up" civil society in order for NGOs and others to act as interest articulators. However, as I demonstrate in Chapters 4 and 5, this is a limited view of the potential NGO contribution to democratization in Africa. The necessity of *empowering* communities to act for themselves rather than relying on NGOs—with their towering resources—to intercede for them is painfully evident from what NGOs identify as the greatest bottleneck to their "political" work.

Local NGOs admit that the greatest impediment to their capacity to be long-term contributors to a vibrant civil society is their dependency on external sources of funding for their operations. Without the generous flow of external funds, most local NGOs would exist only in name. For instance, available evidence suggests that Zimbabwean NGOs depend on external sources of funding for 95 percent of their work (NGO Task Force 1991, 7). This is not an exception. Kenyan NGOs are similarly dependent (Mwangi 1986, cited in Bratton 1989b), and most African NGOs depend as heavily on their Northern partners for operating and project expenses. Apart from raising questions of organizational ownership and autonomy in agenda setting, this extreme dependency seriously undermines NGOs' ability to advance political issues in the long term. Given that even NGO funding has conditions (mostly on project type), a local NGO's agenda may become blurred by that of its donors. And on numerous occasions, African governments have questioned—rather legitimately—whose agendas local NGOs pursue (see Antrobus 1987).

The project-based mode of financing that is more or less the norm in NGO funding makes long-term undertakings in grassroots empowerment even more insecure (Antrobus 1987; Fowler 1991b; NGO Task Force 1991). With this external dependency, there is also the danger—seemingly unlikely, but not improbable—that just as the pre-dominant thinking on the state's developmental potential shifted in the last decade, the present unmitigated hopes placed on NGOs could erode. It is this dependency, rather than government controls, that poses the greatest threat to *organizational* sustainability, which in turn diminishes the potential for NGOs to "pluralize" civil society (Bratton 1989a; Barkan, McNulty, and Ayeni 1991; Chazan 1992; Diamond, Linz, and Lipset 1988; Fowler 1991b). If they do not exist, they cannot pluralize!

African NGOs contribute to the overall process of democratization at two levels. First, NGOs pluralize the civil society environment and may pursue actions that enable them and others to operate more freely and unfettered by the state. As such, NGOs help "enlarge" and "safe-guard" (Kinyanjui 1989) this space that the postindependence African state had eroded. Second, NGOs contribute to the process of democra-tic development by empowering grassroots communities where they pursue their development activities. These communities may then act through these NGOs or independently as politically conscious citi-zens. Much of what has been written on the contribution of NGOs to democratization in Africa relates to the former. Less explored, perhaps because it is less exposed, is the area of grassroots empowerment by NGOs. Given the extreme dependency of local NGOs on their external supporters, their contributions to grassroots empowerment may be more sustainable than their (possibly) short-term occupation as inter-est articulators either for themselves as organizations or as intermedi-aries for their grassroots constituencies. This is not to suggest, however, that NGO efforts to pluralize civil society are less significant than grassroots empowerment. Indeed, it would not be possible to pursue the empowerment goal if an enabling environment for NGO development activities did not exist. This enabling environment is best secured by an active and unfettered civil society, to which NGOs' pluralizing efforts may be crucial. But having secured this enabling environment, NGOs' pursuit of limited "pure development" or "mod-ernization" projects (Fowler 1991b) would fall short of fundamentally altering the life conditions of their grassroots communities.

Civil Society and the State in Kenya

The political context of NGOs in Kenya in the 1980s can be viewed as part of a broader assault on organizations in civil society by a regime seeking to consolidate power and neutralize potential independent agents of agitation. When Kenya's first president Jomo Kenyatta died in 1978, he was succeeded by his long-serving vice president Daniel arap Moi. As a member of the minority Kalenjin community, Moi immediately embarked on efforts to consolidate his precarious position in a state and economy that were dominated by the Kikuyu ethnic group of the former president. Espousing widely populist ideals, such as combating the endemic corruption associated with Kenyatta's patronage system, Moi instilled confidence with a vague but, at the time, reassuring *Nyayo* "philosophy," committing himself to follow Kenyatta's footsteps and retaining the Kikuyu economist Mwai Kibaki as vice president and finance minister (Khapoya 1980).

At the same time, Moi set about dismantling civic and political organizations and networks of patronage that had served Kenyatta's regime and had the potential to undermine his power (Throup 1987). In 1980, Moi banned ethnic welfare associations, a step ostensibly targeted at the Gikuyu Embu Meru Association (GEMA), the largest ethnic association led by prominent old guards of the Kenyatta regime. In 1976, GEMA had spearheaded an attempt to amend the constitution to prevent Moi from automatically assuming the presidency upon Kenyatta's death (Karimi and Ochieng 1980). Moi's consolidation efforts did not begin to affect other societal organizations until he maneuvered the constitutional change that outlawed opposition parties and established the Kenya African National Union (KANU) as the sole political party in June 1982. The move to a de jure single-party state was important to civil society organizations; it shifted the arena of state-society relations to the party apparatus and cut off the state-society links that such organizations had established in the Kenyatta era as somewhat independent, if malleable, organs of patronage. As Moi rejuvenated the party with an eye to building an independent patronage network loyal to him, these organizations were unlikely to be beneficiaries, since he saw them as challengers (Widner 1992; Barkan and Chege 1989; Barkan 1992).

It is in the single-party years that state-society relations showed particular strain. Mutahi Ngunyi and Kamau Gathiaka (1993) identify six distinct "trajectories" of state-society relations in the context of the single-party regime in Kenya. As a consequence of KANU's drive for hegemony, societal organizations were (1) deregistered or proscribed, (2) "beheaded" or "emasculated" by forcing the removal of leaders or withdrawing resources and privileges, (3) reconstituted into new organizations by governmental fiat, (4) forced to withdraw or diminish contacts with the state to avoid antagonism, (5) co-opted by the state, or (6) openly opposed to the single party (Ngunyi and Gathiaka 1993, 8–13; see also Widner 1992, ch. 6).

Organizations that were disbanded included the Matatu Vehicle Owners Association, the Public Service Club, the University Staff Union, and the Student Organization of the University of Nairobi. The first three, as preserves of the Kikuyu commercial transport, civil service, and university elite, were potential opposition strongholds; the university students had already rioted, most notably in support of an attempted coup in August 1982. University lecturers were also subjected to constant harassment after the coup attempt, and some had been detained or exiled.[1] Other organizations, particularly farmers' organizations that had been favored by the Kenyatta patronage network and whose deregistration would have undermined immediate economic prospects, were "beheaded" or otherwise weakened. For instance, the Kenya Farmers Association, which had a virtual monopoly over farming inputs, was dissolved and reconstituted as the Kenya Grain Growers Cooperative Union in 1984 under a new leadership. The influential Kenya Coffee Planters Union and the Kenya Tea Development Authority were both reorganized by the state at various times in the 1980s (Ngethe and Odero 1992).

The government also created other organizations, especially cooperatives in marginal areas, as avenues of patronage to regions and groups that had not benefited from Kenyatta's regime (Ngunyi and Gathiaka 1993; Barkan and Chege 1989). Other established groups continued to exist and function without conflict with the regime so long as they acquiesced to regime preferences. For example, the Federation of Kenya Employers continued cooperative consultations with the government in tightly controlled labor relations favoring employers (*Weekly Review,* May 23, 1987). In 1987, the KANU government co-opted *Maendeleo ya Wanawake,* the national women's organization, whose leadership had already been dissolved by the government, without any legal basis, because of a financial scandal (*Weekly Review,* May 7, 1987, 11–12). In 1990, the Central Organization of Trade Unions (COTU) voluntarily linked itself to the party for a short time in an attempt to formalize its already diminutive position in labor issues.

Throughout the 1980s, two organizations resisted attempts by the KANU government to control them and later emerged as the major opposition voices in a civil society cowed by the single party. The Law Society of Kenya, a professional organization of over 1,500 lawyers that had been politically dormant for most of its existence, became more outspoken in the late 1980s, in large part due to a radicalized leadership tied to displaced political elites from the former government. The second organization that emerged as an active opponent to the single-party regime was the National Council of Churches of Kenya (NCCK), the main umbrella body for Protestant churches. The NCCK had been an active agitator during the independence movement but had been mute during much of the postindependence period. The activism by these two organizations was so intense in the late 1980s that, in the absence of political parties, they became the unofficial "opposition" to the KANU hegemony.

These organizations opposed further steps by the single-party regime to remove or weaken many of the legal institutions guaranteeing government accountability. For instance, in 1986, the KANU government abolished the secret ballot in party and national elections under the pretext that an open queuing system (where voters lined up behind their favored candidate) would be less prone to rigging. The NCCK vehemently opposed this action, citing the obvious danger of voter intimidation. Similarly, when the government removed the security of tenure that guaranteed some measure of independence for the attorney general, the auditor general, and high court judges (all of whom would then serve at the president's pleasure), the Law Society of Kenya led the opposition to this move that would undermine checks on state actions. Although the government did not acquiesce to opposition from these organizations, their actions were noteworthy in that outside the single-party parliament, which had been reduced to a "rubber-stamp body," these organizations became the vehicles for early agitation from within civil society for political change.

Among nonreligious development NGOs, only the Green Belt Movement under Wangari Maathai emerged as an outspoken critic of the single-party regime. Maathai's open opposition to plans to convert a public park in Nairobi into an office complex in 1989 was a highly unusual event, since many NGOs eschewed direct involvement in the political arena. Maathai's own relations with the Moi regime, including a frustrated parliamentary bid in 1979, contributed to the organization's abandonment of the self-restraint that was characteristic of NGOs in the 1980s. Maathai's challenge to the single party included an unsuccessful civil suit against the state that earned her scathing personal attacks from parliament and the president and contributed to the regime's impetus to control NGOs (*Daily Nation*, December 9–24, 1989).

Opposition against the KANU government was also spearheaded by individuals occupying resourceful positions and having a commanding voice in civil society. For instance, prominent clerics such as Reverend Alexander Kipsang Muge, Reverend Timothy Njoya, and Bishop Henry Okullu emerged as crusaders against government corruption and repression, even as their own church hierarchies remained mute or, in the case of Njoya, hostile.[2] The private press gave prominent and sympathetic coverage to controversial sermons by these clerics. Similarly, a number of news publications with political agendas sympathetic to political pluralism thrived and met state repression, including confiscation of numerous issues and outright banning. For instance, the government proscribed *Beyond* in 1988, *Financial Review* and *Development Agenda* in 1989, and the *Nairobi Law Monthly* in 1990.[3] Such visible confrontations chipped steadily at the state's legitimacy.

A succession of events in 1990 and 1991 provided the sparks that ignited the opposition fire, eventually leading to multiparty pluralism. In February 1990, Minister for Foreign Affairs Robert Ouko was found murdered after being missing for two days. This led to mass demonstrations and riots in Nairobi and Kisumu as initial evidence and rumors suggested government complicity in the assassination. In July 1991, a pressure group called the Forum for the Restoration of Democracy (FORD) was formed, bringing together prominent multiparty activists and displaced politicians. As an informal body requiring no legal registration, FORD became the vehicle through which further agitation for party pluralism was conducted. On its part, the KANU government continued its onslaught against multiparty advocates: arresting and detaining opponents and journalists and forcefully suppressing mass action. In what became a watershed event, in July 1991, the government detained two prominent politicians who had resigned from the government and had planned a mass rally in support of multiparty politics. Riots ensued when armed police fired to disperse the crowd that had gathered for the mass meeting, killing twenty-eight people (Barkan 1993). In response to the widespread demands for reform and in hopes of controlling the process, the government appointed the KANU Review Committee, which held public hearings on how the party could reform to accommodate dissent (*Weekly Review,* July 27, 1990, 3–6).

The increasing human rights abuses and repression of political opponents by the Kenyan government also elicited external condemnation, particularly from major development aid donors such as the United States, Britain, and Germany. The most visible and immediate donor pressure came from then U.S. ambassador Smith Hempstone, who openly criticized the government's repression of its opponents. In November 1991, the major donors to Kenya suspended aid until the government legalized multiparty politics and held multiparty elections. In the hope of unfreezing much-needed aid and placating advocates of political pluralism, President Moi announced in December 1991 that KANU would ask parliament to amend the constitution to legalize opposition parties. In December 1992, multiparty elections were held and, although Moi and KANU retained the presidency and a majority in parliament, for the first time since 1964, there were opposition parties in parliament. The elections themselves were marred by complaints of rigging and other irregularities, including ethnic clashes in opposition strongholds in which the government was implicated. Even after the elections, withheld aid was not released until late 1993, and subsequent disbursements have been tied not only to required changes in the economy but also to governance reforms, including steps to eliminate corruption and to allow opposition parties and civil society organizations to operate without interference from the government.

This broad assault on civil society by the single-party state was the context in which Kenyan NGOs operated throughout the 1980s. However, it was not until the late 1980s that NGOs became targets of direct state control, culminating in the NGO Coordination Act of 1990. In reaction to these attempts to control them, NGOs became one of the various actors opposing the single-party government on diverse issues and lent further momentum to the democratization movement unfolding in the early 1990s. Given the outcomes of previous conflicts between the Kenyan government and societal organizations, it was unexpected that NGOs would prevail in opposing the NGO legislation. How and why they prevailed to ensure an "enabling environment" for their operations and how this became part of the evolving democratization movement is the subject of the next chapter.

Notes

1. On the Matatu Vehicle Owners Association and other transport groups, see *Weekly Review,* December 9, 1988, pp. 13–14, and December 16, 1988, pp. 21–22; on relations between the state and university students and faculty, see, for example, *Weekly Review,* December 4, 1987, pp. 27–28; April 11, 1986, pp. 4–6; and February 15, 1985, pp. 3–13.
2. On relations between the government and churches or individual clerics, see, for example, *Weekly Review,* September 4, 1987, pp. 3–7; December 8, 1989, pp. 8–10; and February 3, 1989, pp. 4–10.
3. On government-press relations, see, for example, *Weekly Review,* January 26, 1990, pp. 17–18; March 30, 1990, pp. 16–18; March 27, 1992, p. 16; March 18, 1988, pp. 18–19; and October 5, 1990, pp. 21–23.

3

NGOs and the State
in Kenya

IN DECEMBER 1990, the Kenyan government passed the NGO Coordination Act with the express purpose of controlling the activities of NGOs in the country. Over the next two years, this legislation became the focal point of NGO-state relations as NGOs collectively fought government control. This confrontation was among the most prominent challenges mounted by civil society organizations against the single-party state in Kenya. It is a case that elaborates the state-society tension and offers important lessons for the theory of civil society's role in democratization. This incident provides sound support for the civil society–democratization thesis: it shows civil society actors opposing the repressive state and pursuing actions that have important bearings on political reform in Kenya. Moreover, it reveals civil society actors that are politically conscious and have taken advantage of opportunities and resources within the broader democratization movement. The eventual success of the NGO challenge itself had important implications for the political reform movement: it allowed NGOs to operate freely and independently from state interference—thus increasing the freedom of actors in civil society—and it allowed some NGOs (for example, the Green Belt Movement) to pursue more forthright political actions with a reduced risk of being outlawed.

A close examination of this incident is important for three reasons. First, it clearly illustrates the tensions between state and society as suggested in the literature on state–civil society relations. In particular, it highlights the contentiousness of the development arena in Kenya, which led to government attempts to control NGOs. Second, it elaborates the process of such conflict, emphasizing the evolution of conflict as opposed to automatic submission. Third, it suggests factors that enabled NGOs to triumph in this conflict and that may be applicable to other civil society–state conflicts in Africa.

31

The last two reasons reflect two gaps that remain in the current understanding of civil society's role in political change. The first gap is that no attention has been given to the struggles of civil society organizations to exist and operate freely in the presence of an intimidating state. There has been no systematic study of such struggles or of the process through which civil society actors reassert their independence. Instead, the focus has been on actions of civil society organizations that already have some latitude for political action and pursue such actions in collective attempts to redefine the political system. However, such forthright political actions can be pursued only after securing the necessary latitude for independent action. The case of NGOs in Kenya illustrates the process of civil society's challenge to an intimidating state.

The second gap in present theorizing is a lack of identification of the factors that facilitate civil society's reassertion and contributions to political reform movements. Since civil society's existence and oppositional actions are not new but were previously suppressed by autocratic states, it is necessary for analysts to explain why civil society has lately become the arena from which effective challenges to the state have been launched. It is crucial to understand the causes of this efficacy. In the case of NGOs in Kenya, I highlight four factors that are important to the success of NGO opposition to the state. These singular factors have greater explanatory power when they converge in a situation, which may explain why earlier attempts to force African governments to liberalize their political systems failed when a combination of the four factors could not be mustered.

Previous studies that document incidents of state repression of NGOs indicate little or no opposition from NGOs. It is assumed that the NGOs meekly submitted to the repressive environment. Of late, however, attempts to control NGOs have also presented opportunities to oppose the state at a time when resources and international goodwill are tilted in favor of nonstate actors. I suggest that instead of the submission assumed in the snapshots that other analysts have provided, NGOs have reacted to government control in three progressive steps, when conditions have permitted: from initial attempts to adjust and seek amicable coexistence with authoritarian regimes, to more outright opposition and agitation against repression, and finally, to sanctions to force states to adjust their control over the NGO sector.

LAnd Labour
Land Tenure
Resource Allocation
Local Knowledge

Tensions between NGOs and the State

As early as 1986, the Kenyan government was concerned about the burgeoning NGO sector. By then, the government was well aware of the evolving donor preference for NGOs over developing country governments as agents of development administration (see Oyugi 1986). Recognizing that NGOs would set their own priorities that might collectively prove to be diverse and wayward from its own development plans, the Kenyan government sought to "coordinate" and direct them toward its own vision of state-coordinated development. Thus, a ranking government official—the permanent secretary in the office of the president in charge of internal security and arguably one of the most powerful officials at the time—remarked to NGOs in 1986:

> When you have 350 or so bodies all active in one aspect or other of a country's development, you run the danger of losing sight of the main challenges of development and much duplication of effort. . . . Where resources are limited, as is the case in this country and other third world nations, to be meaningful, development must involve planning the utilization of available resources to achieve agreed social and economic goals. (Oyugi 1986, 5)

The solution was therefore "planning in context" or coordination. This coordination was to be effected by requiring all NGOs to liaise with local district development committees (DDCs), which were ostensibly the grassroots decision-making bodies. In reality, however, DDCs were effectively controlled by the central government: committee membership was restricted to politicians from the single party (KANU), and committees were chaired by district commissioners, who were presidential appointees under the docket of provincial administration and internal security. It is with such DDCs that NGOs were required to clear their projects and budgets. At the national level, they were required to clear the same with relevant ministries, especially the Ministry of Finance and the Ministry of Planning, so that these projects could be noted in the government's development record (Republic of Kenya 1989). In effect, this meant that NGO projects became "government" projects, making them potential pork for political patronage. *Accountability Mechanism — wave software.*

Although these initial overtures were couched in the language of "coordination" for the sake of development, their origin in the executive arm overseeing internal security rather than development planning was foreboding. Indeed, the most forceful calls for NGO coordination were made in response to opposition by the National Council of Churches of Kenya (NCCK) to the queue-voting method introduced by KANU to replace the secret ballot for the country's elections. The NCCK's stand against KANU was roundly condemned by party stalwarts, who called for more stringent controls on both local and foreign NGOs (Omoro 1986; *Weekly Review,* September 19, 1986). Previously, President Moi had announced that future NGO funding would have to be channeled through the government (*Daily Nation,* September 10, 1986). In December 1986, he underlined his commitment to rein in NGOs by charging that some NGOs were involved in "subversive" activities (*Daily Nation,* December 14, 1986). Moi's call for greater state control of NGOs had snowballing but somewhat erratic effects. In January 1987, NGOs were required to register with the Ministry of Finance, but the government circular containing this directive was sent to only seventy NGOs whose addresses the government knew. This in itself was a major indication of the government's lack of control over the sector—there were over 400 operating NGOs. The information required in this registration included names of senior officers, project location, and source of funds and projected expenditures from 1986 to 1991.

Meanwhile, the NGO community was well aware of its uncoordinated state and the adverse effects this had on its shared goals. The sectoral disarray was reflected by NGOs' duplication of work, reinvention of solutions, and general lack of information exchange (KNCSS 1989). A more important indication of their disorganization was the fact that less than half of them were members of their umbrella body, the Kenya National Council of Social Services (KNCSS), in existence since 1963. This situation was partly a result of the different arrangements under which NGOs could operate in the country, which gave them different legal identities. Most NGOs were registered under the Societies Act and were placed under the Ministry of Culture and Social Services—thus the KNCSS umbrella body. However, many others operated under the Companies Act, the Trustee Act, or other protocol arrangements with the Ministry of Foreign Affairs or Ministry of Planning. Moreover, their privileges and services were administered by scattered agencies, such as the immigration and customs departments. This situation made it difficult for NGOs to perceive themselves as one community, and they remained unorganized and inarticulate. But as the state's threats to their hitherto unfettered operations increased, NGOs undertook efforts to diffuse imminent government control.

In 1989, President Moi announced that the government would create a directorate to coordinate NGOs and ensure that their activities were compatible with national interests (*The Standard,* October 24, 1992). Pending the creation of the NGO directorate, the registration of new NGOs was severely restricted, as were services traditionally offered to the sector, for example, duty-free imports of equipment and entry and work permits for expatriate staff (*Daily Nation,* August 19, 1988; Fowler 1991a). Inter-NGO discussions on coordination intensified in late 1989 in apparent reaction to these successive announcements and movements in government indicating that work was under way to establish the NGO directorate and draft legislation according to the president's directive (see Njiru 1989, 6). In a seminar organized by the KNCSS and the Institute for Development Studies, one of the policy research arms of the University of Nairobi, NGOs came up with proposals on how best to coordinate their activities and facilitate their development work (KNCSS 1989; Waruhiu 1989). These proposals were later presented by the KNCSS to an interministerial team working on the NGO legislation. This team brought together the traditional ministries involved in NGO work and development planning and the now ubiquitous Office of the President. The NGO proposals were a preemptive attempt to forestall stringent government controls that seemed imminent from the strong condemnatory statements that the NGOs had been subjected to. At this time, NGOs could not be assertive not only because they remained feebly organized but also because the national political context (under a repressive single party already agitated by NGOs) would not bear more assertive actions. The more politically palatable options, as indicated in discussions within the KNCSS, were limited to open commitments to work with the government, register themselves, consult with local DDCs and relevant ministries, and work toward more amicable self-government (see KNCSS 1989).

At the same time, a fiery confrontation between the government and the Green Belt Movement (GBM) underscored the political imperative of controlling NGOs and triggered concerted efforts to rein in the NGO sector through legislation. In 1989, the KANU government cordoned off part of Uhuru Park, the only public park in the center of Nairobi. The purpose was to build a sixty-story media complex that would have been the largest structure of its kind in Africa. The GBM vehemently opposed this project as environmentally unsound, since it would destroy one of the surviving green spots in the city and would also deny thousands of city residents their recreational facilities. The NGO proceeded to sue the government and lobby the project's external financiers to drop their sponsorship of the complex unless the environmental implications were adequately addressed (*Weekly Review,* December 15, 1989). Predictably, these actions provoked the wrath of the government and party politicians, including the president, who condemned the GBM and called for its deregistration and for more stringent controls on NGOs in general (see *Daily Nation,* November 9–24, 1989).

This confrontation pushed NGOs into the political limelight, and their "coordination" became an even more urgent concern for the government. Behind the scenes, in a rather unremarkable event in a single-party state, Office of the President personnel hijacked the drafting of the legislation (Fowler 1991a; NGOSC 1991b). From the subsequent bill, it was clear that the KNCSS recommendations presented to the interministerial panel working on the NGO legislation had been largely sidelined. The much-publicized GBM-KANU fight over the Uhuru Park complex had predictably convulsed the legislation process. For instance, from the various inconsistencies and inadequacies in the subsequent bill, legal experts were of the considered opinion that it was not the work of experienced legal draftspersons but was rather hurriedly drafted to respond to the political exigencies of the day rather than to the need for facilitating NGO development initiatives (Jaffer 1991).

In November 1990, the NGO Coordination Bill was published and introduced in parliament and then suddenly withdrawn without reason. It was reintroduced in December, a few days before parliament would adjourn for the long Christmas recess. Within two days, the bill had been rushed through the required readings, debated, and passed. It now required only presidential assent to become law. The speed with which the bill was passed reflects the "rubber-stamp" role that parliament played in the single-party state.[1] In the parliamentary debate, NGOs came under severe criticism for overrunning the country and "operating outside the system"—essentially challenging the system under which the single-party state was the supreme authority and development machine. None of the recorded contributions espoused the positive contributions NGOs made to the country's development or the need for coordination to facilitate their work, which was the government's official raison d'être for the legislation. The common theme of members' contributions was the need to "control" NGOs. In his concluding remarks as the sponsor of the bill, Minister of State Burudi Nabwera stated: "Once the Board is established no NGO will be allowed to operate outside the system. If an NGO engages in activities inimical to the country, it will be de-registered. An organization like Green Belt Movement will be expected to plant trees and not engage in other [political] things" (*Daily Nation,* December 14, 1990).

From the preceding, some impressions are worth noting. The Kenyan government was aware of the increasing flow of development aid to NGOs instead of to the state. The state's diminishing development resources would undermine its capacity for political patronage or legitimation. Compounding this implicit political challenge was the more explicit political criticism that the larger, older, and more internationally connected NGOs (for example, NCCK and GBM)[2] were willing to level against the single-party state. Ostensibly, the two organizations (as does much of the NGO sector in Kenya) also reflected the interests of central province ethnic groups and elites, which were the groups Moi had successfully displaced as dominant political players after succeeding Kenyatta in 1978. In light of the ethnic-laden politics of Kenya, efforts by any group in civil society cannot escape shades of ethnic meanings being ascribed to them by observers or by the main protagonists. Similarly, this situation conditions much of the response from the state—itself both an arena for and the subject of ethnic competition.

In addition, the personality dimension cannot be ignored. For instance, the GBM-KANU fight over the planned skyscraper at Uhuru Park was transformed into a personal battle between President Moi and Wangari Maathai, the GBM coordinator. This revolt by the GBM seems to have convulsed the government's efforts to regulate NGOs. The single-party state was known to institute legislation or policy to counter specific individuals,[3] and the importance of the personality dimension was most apparent in the "hijack" of the drafting of the legislation by the Office of the President staff after the Moi-Maathai spat.

It is also apparent that as a community, NGOs in Kenya were unable to influence the legislation process, primarily because they remained disorganized, which lessened their capacity to be assertive. This disorganized state was not due to NGOs' lack of organizational ability (this they had) but because to organize outright political crusades in the single-party context, especially when the regime was agitated, was to risk being shut down. The fact that the NCCK and GBM could do this was testimony to their near "untouchable" nature.[4]

The NGO Legislation

Although fundamentally flawed, the NGO Act provided an institutional framework for NGO operations. First and foremost, it provided a single law that would govern the whole sector, rather than the varied legal regimes under which NGOs previously operated. It thus gave them a recognized legal status, with a standard legal definition as corporate bodies. It also established an executive directorate, called the NGO Bureau, which would oversee the administration of the NGO sector, including registration and coordination; established an NGO Board, which was the government-NGO policy- and decision-making body (to which the NGO Bureau was the executive directorate); and provided for NGO self-government through a National Council of Voluntary Agencies. Despite these provisions, NGOs were extremely alarmed by the act. They saw it not as enabling legislation that would facilitate their activities but as a law that would control and constrain their work. The parliamentary debate on the bill had betrayed the government's intentions to control NGOs in the name of coordination. This was further borne out by the specific provisions of the bill: the composition of the NGO Board was heavily in favor of the government; the powers of the board were wide and far-reaching; the operations of the council (the NGO self-governing body) were not independent from government interference; the minister in charge of the NGO sector was granted absolute powers, and no recourse to the courts was provided for NGOs; and the administering authority was under the internal security, not the development planning, department (see Republic of Kenya 1990b).[5]

NGO Reaction to the Legislation

NGO reaction to the legislation took shape in three distinct steps, starting with a fairly innocuous informational meeting and quickly progressing to collective organization and face-to-face lobbying with high-ranking government officials and eventually to intense confrontations with the government. These events suggest three stages of confronting the state: (1) adjusting to repression, (2) mounting opposition, and (3) instigating sanctions to force the state to adjust.

Step 1

In January 1991, the president signed the NGO Act into law. What remained to make the law operational was the drafting of subsidiary legislation (rules and regulations) and a notice of commencement by the minister in charge. The president's action transformed the situation into a crisis for NGOs, which were still discussing the law informally. In February 1991, the Institute for Development Studies (IDS) organized a seminar for NGOs to familiarize themselves with the new law. IDS had long been involved with NGOs and with the government in research and policy matters and had been instrumental in the 1989

NGO Concerns about the Legislation

Among the major concerns expressed by NGOs at their first meeting on the legislation were the following:

1. The government's intention: The intention of the act was suspect; although it was couched in the language of facilitation and coordination, which were welcome goals, the act actually controlled and constrained NGOs through the board, whose membership was heavily weighted in the government's favor.

2. The minister's power: The act bestowed absolute power on the minister in charge of determining the affairs of NGOs, such as registration, deregistration, duty exemption, work permits, and so forth. All appeals were to be made to this minister, whose decision would be final. Most important, no recourse to courts of law was provided.

3. Registration period: The act required NGOs to renew their registration certificates every five years. In effect, this limited the life span of NGOs to five years at a time. NGOs believed that this would adversely affect their operations, especially planning and resource procurement. Moreover, there was no guarantee that new terms and conditions would not be introduced at the renewal stage.

4. Deregistration: The act empowered the board to suspend or deregister an NGO for the actions of its officers. NGOs considered this to be too punitive, since closing down an NGO would have widespread adverse effects, and to do so on account of an individual's action was excessive. Also, there was no formal mechanism for appeal except to the minister—essentially to the same government that would have "apprehended, prosecuted, and punished" the NGO.

5. Self-government: The act provided for the establishment of a National Council of Voluntary Agencies (presumably to replace the KNCSS) whose membership would be limited to the first 100 NGOs whose registration was approved by the board. This council would then draft a code of conduct to be approved by the minister that would be binding for all NGOs. NGOs thought that the council should be elected by *all* NGOs and that democratic principles should be followed in its operations. Its decisions should not require further approval from the government.

6. The relations, rights, and obligations between the board and the council needed to be clarified.

7. Financing the law's operation: The attorney general's memorandum accompanying the bill had explicitly stated that the exchequer would not incur any additional expense for the administration of the law. The NGOs wanted to know if they would then be required to finance the executive bureau's operations.

8. Transitional arrangements: The status of previous privileges (for example, duty exemption), as well as the operating status of many NGOs under protocol arrangements, was unclear.

9. Definitions: Many of the act's definitions were vague. For example, it was unclear whether churches and self-help groups and donor organizations without projects were classified as NGOs. (See NGOSC 1991a.)

KNCSS workshop on coordination. The February seminar was attended by representatives of over 130 NGOs and ranking government officials, including one who later became the executive director of the new NGO Coordination Bureau. The purpose of the seminar was purely to educate the NGOs on the act, its requirements, and its implications for their work. Aware of the political constraints in seeking to influence "control" policy in a single-party regime, neither the international development agencies that funded the seminar nor the IDS policy analysts who organized it harbored any illusions that NGOs could successfully pressure for changes in the legislation. Indeed, Alan Fowler, one of the foremost observers of the NGO scene in Kenya, wrote in an aide-mémoire to NGOs: "Given the parliamentarians' response to the Bill it is highly unlikely that it will be repealed or amended on the basis of strong NGO lobbying. A more important and practical response therefore, is to try and influence the regulations defining the actual operation of the Bureau" (1991a, 5).

However, NGO discussions at the seminar revealed deep and widespread displeasure with the act, and NGO representatives sought more fundamental changes than merely influencing the rules and regulations that were currently being drafted. NGO representatives argued that the legislation was "controlling" rather than regulatory or "facilitatory" (NGOSC 1991a, 3). During this one sitting, NGO representatives would move from a familiar mode of adjustment to state repression to one of organized agitation for amicable conditions for their work in development.

Step 2

The transformation from the traditional attitude of adjusting to state control to lobbying and opposing such control was swift. The 130 NGOs at the February 1991 workshop resolved to pressure the government to examine their concerns and rectify the legislation. Recognizing the necessity for collective organization (and given the nebulous legal status of the KNCSS), NGOs constituted themselves into the NGO Network—a body organized for the sole purpose of discussing NGO concerns regarding the legislation and making representations to the government. To facilitate this goal, the network elected a ten-member NGO Standing Committee (NGOSC) with the mandate to make representations to the government on behalf of Network members and report back to them (NGOSC 1991e).

It is instructive to note that the ten members elected to the Standing Committee included leading figures in the NGO sector and representatives of major foreign and local NGOs. The leading personalities who also headed or represented large and influential NGOs included Ezra Mbogori, director of the Undugu Society of Kenya; Dr. Njuguna Ngethe, director of the Institute for Development Studies; Achoka Awori, director of the Kenya Energy and Environment NGO (KENGO); and Dr. John Batten, director of Action Aid in Kenya. Other influential NGOs represented included the NCCK, the Aga Khan Foundation, FEMNET (a women's rights NGO), and *Kituo cha Sheria* (a high-profile legal advisory center and an active proponent of political pluralism). The members of the Standing Committee represented the largest NGOs; they had years of experience working with the government and had direct contacts with government officials. The NGOSC included some of the more assertive NGOs and collectively controlled immense development resources, which gave them voice and public and media attention. But even with such leverage, the political context precluded any forceful pressure, since the government could proscribe the network and its constituent units. The present opportunity allowed only for careful negotiation with the government. This Standing Committee was therefore mandated to establish a dialogue with the government, present the concerns and resolutions of the network to the Office of the President, and make recommendations on the act and the rules to be formulated (NGOSC 1991a, 4).

In March 1991, the NGOSC met ranking government officials from various ministries, led by those of the Office of the President, and presented NGO concerns about the act. The presentation included a document comprising the preliminary report of the February IDS-NGO seminar, a document enumerating NGO general concerns, a document detailing these concerns and recommendations on the act section by section, and a draft bill synthesizing the NGO suggestions (see NGOSC 1991a). In the four-hour-long meeting at the Office of the President, the government officials sought to dispel any illusions that the act would be amended and encouraged the NGOs to instead contribute to the rule-making exercise already under way. However, in the ensuing discussion and debate, the NGOSC exposed many issues that the government officials conceded were legitimate and needed to be addressed (NGOSC 1991c). Despite their insistence that the act had already been enacted and that the question of amendments was therefore moot, the government officials gave encouraging signs that the government was open to further consultations with NGOs. Indeed, they strategically asserted that this initial meeting was a "continuation of government-NGO dialogue" and, by implication, that the NGO legislation was a product of previous dialogue. Of course, the NGOSC was aware this was the first such consultative meeting (NGOSC 1991c).

The NGOSC reported back to the NGO Network in a second workshop held in mid-April that was attended by over 130 NGO representatives. Although most network members commended the achievements of the NGOSC and were particularly appreciative of the government's willingness to dialogue, many expressed doubts that verbal concessions on the inadequacies of the act would amount to much. They did not want their concerns to be dismissed as wrinkles in the legislation that could be ironed out later. Instead, they wanted them addressed more concretely through amendments to the act. The network unanimously agreed that the implementation of the act as it stood would adversely affect their independence and operations and, consequently, their grassroots constituents. They would therefore press for the necessary amendments to correct the situation before the act was implemented. To this end, they resolved and mandated the Standing Committee to request the government to delay the implementation of the act until the NGO concerns were resolved and halt the drafting of the rules until these concerns were resolved (NGOSC 1991f).

In addition, NGOs sought to build a broader alliance with other resourceful and interested parties. The NGOSC sought the main Western donors' views on the act to find out if they could intercede for NGOs if current efforts did not result in favorable amendments. To this end, the Standing Committee met representatives of major donor agencies (USAID, UNEP, UNDP, UNICEF, the Ford Foundation, and the World Bank, among others). The donor representatives expressed both concern about the legislation and support for the network's efforts. On their part, the donors (through their subcommittee on NGOs) urged the Kenyan government to respond favorably to NGO concerns by making amendments to the legislation. Although NGOs would not request donors to lobby on their behalf, they would rely on the donors to back them up, especially in the event of a hostile government reaction, since "donors may facilitate further concessions without the need for NGOs, who are more vulnerable, to light more fires" (NGOSC 1991d, 3).

Furthermore, there was a need for alternative strategies to persuade the government to address NGO concerns if present approaches were rejected. Among the suggestions made to the Standing Committee were the following:

1. Continue to hold a series of roundtable talks with policymakers to discuss the act and make further representations.

2. Push for a national forum at which the government would educate all NGOs about the act; this would also give NGOs an opportunity to forcefully make their concerns known.

3. As a final option in direct dealing with the government, request the president to intervene.

4. Request donors to lobby on NGOs' behalf, since they have greater leverage.

5. Institute court action in the form of an "interpretation suit" that would delay the operationalization of the act.

6. Wait and see what happens with the implementation—some NGOs argued that the government would not be able to effect the legislation because of its limited resources.

7. If all else fails and the act is actually implemented, seek to influence the appointments to the NGO Board, which was the central decision-making body (see NGOSC 1991f, 5–6).

For a number of reasons, most of these options were abandoned as being too confrontational (2, 3, 4, and 5) or likely to be too late to achieve much (3, 6, and 7). The network consistently eschewed confrontation and preferred low-profile lobbying of high-ranking officials. This was essentially a survivalist tactic, even as the NGOs became more organized and more aggressive. The only option open, therefore, was lobbying as they had been doing. Lobbying, they collectively reasoned, "was a legitimate activity that should be undertaken without fear and . . . should be carried out from a wholistic approach which entails utilization of all possible ways and means to achieve underlying objectives" (NGOSC 1991f, 8).

To facilitate an expanded lobbying effort, the network resolved to expand the membership of the NGOSC from ten to twenty. The enlarged Standing Committee was also divided into three subcommittees with specialized tasks: liaison with the government, public education, and rules and regulations. The liaison subcommittee had the responsibility of making representations to the government. The Standing Committee was now mandated to expand its lobbying contacts beyond the Office of the President to the attorney general's office and parliament. The NGOSC would continue to hold consultative meetings with government representatives and pursue NGO concerns "as diplomatically as possible" (NGOSC 1991f, 8). The public education subcommittee would work to educate donors, other NGOs, and particularly the public on the implications of the NGO Act. This would be done through direct contact with donors and NGOs and a media campaign highlighting NGO contributions to development in Kenya. The rules and regulations subcommittee would work on the act's subsidiary legislation proposed by the government to ensure that it addressed NGO concerns as reflected in the NGO version of the act. This specialization is indicative of the increasing organizational acumen that NGOs were displaying in their efforts to pool resources to seek a less threatening environment.

In late May 1991, the NGO Standing Committee received positive indications from the permanent secretary that the government was indeed "taking their observations seriously . . . [and] drafting the appropriate miscellaneous amendments to make [the NGO working] environment even more harmonious" (Republic of Kenya 1991a, 1). These amendments, the communication stated, would be tabled in parliament as soon as it reconvened. Apparently displeased with the parallel pressure that international bodies and foreign government representatives were exerting, the permanent secretary took the opportunity to discourage NGOs from "donor lobbing" (sic), as this would be detrimental to a harmonious working environment (2). The NGOSC duly communicated these positive overtures to its constituents in the network, and the lobbying took a lull as they anticipated the publication of the amendments.

In September 1991, when the government published the Miscellaneous Amendment Bill, which included the intended amendments to the NGO Act, NGOs were shocked. Very few of their concerns had been addressed in the proposed amendments. Only three amendments were considered important by NGOs: (1) the requirement that NGOs should renew their registration every five years was dropped, thus granting NGOs corporate status with perpetual succession; (2) the provision that the first 100 NGOs registered would form the NGO Council was amended so that they would form only an interim council (the council's name was also changed to the National Council of NGOs, rather than Voluntary Agencies); and (3) the NGO Board's power to "suspend" was retracted, but not the greater power to deregister an NGO. The other major amendments suggested by the NGOs were completely sidestepped (see Republic of Kenya 1991b).

An urgent third national workshop for the NGO Network was hurriedly convened in October 1991, at which over seventy NGOs were represented. While expressing appreciation for the concessions already made by the government, the network did not hide the fact that it expected and would press for more amendments. Problems such as the absolute powers of the minister, the NGO Board's composition, registration requirements and punitive deregistration, and the question of how the NGO Bureau's operations would be financed were yet to be addressed. Furthermore, adding urgency to the situation, the government presented the network with the draft rules for comment—which indicated the government's intention to implement the law despite outstanding NGO concerns (NGOSC 1991g).

Realizing that the dialogue with the Office of the President had not borne fair fruit, the NGO Standing Committee turned to the attorney general's office, which would move the amendments through parliament and might see the necessity of addressing the NGO concerns.[6] In its meeting with the attorney general, the NGOSC expressed the network's dissatisfaction with the published amendments that fell short of their requests and were disappointing in light of what had seemed to be positive indications from the highest levels of the president's office. NGOs indicated their intention to pursue more vigorous lobbying, especially of lawmakers, to ensure that more favorable amendments were passed. The attorney general reiterated the government's commitment to providing an "enabling environment" to NGOs and promised to "slip" the overlooked amendments into the amendment bill when it was tabled in parliament (NGOSC 1991h). Given that whatever the attorney general tabled in parliament would pass in its entirety, the NGOSC dropped its high-profile tactic of lobbying lawmakers. The attorney general's promise was duly communicated to network members in a fourth national workshop in November (NGOSC 1991h).

When the Miscellaneous Amendment Bill was tabled in parliament in December 1991, NGOs were once again shocked that it did not include their suggested amendments. The attorney general had been "unable" to slip in the more favorable amendments, and the bill was passed as previously published. It seemed that all efforts to lobby for changes in the act had fallen on deaf ears, and the NGOs had been able to achieve only limited success. NGOs were particularly incensed by this turn of events, given that Kenya was undergoing fundamental changes toward political pluralism, which was expected to open up civil society (NGOSC 1992b). Indeed, throughout the lobbying period, the single-party regime had been slowly crumbling under the onslaught of multiparty advocates. Moved by sporadic riots and the suspension of aid by the Paris Club in November 1991, the Kenyan government repealed the section of the constitution that outlawed opposition parties in December 1991. The political context had changed, and the prevailing fluidity presented an opportunity for NGOs to demand a more favorable working environment. NGOs saw the recent developments regarding the NGO Act as a contradiction of this new phase of political reform that expanded the opportunity for independent political action. The besieged condition of the single-party dictatorship emboldened NGOs to challenge it to retract this overbearing statute. Furthermore, the network had received funding and other support from major donors to set up a secretariat and to underwrite the costs of the continuing lobbying exercise. This donor support as well as the government's own recognition of the network as the de facto representative of NGOs went a long way to institutionalize and strengthen its lobbying efforts.

Step 3

Given the government's recent moves ignoring NGO concerns, the NGO Standing Committee called another urgent meeting in February 1992 for NGOs to map out a new strategy. At this fifth national workshop, over 200 NGOs were represented—suggesting the growing concern about the recent turn of events and a willingness to mount challenges against the state. In this charged atmosphere, NGOs radically changed their accommodative stand of lobbying for amendments, they now sought to have the law repealed altogether. Furthermore, they refused to contribute to the draft subsidiary legislation that they had received for comment from the government, arguing that it was useless to make rules and regulations for legislation that was fundamentally flawed. This collective decision to reject the legislation was duly communicated to the Office of the President and to the attorney general. The NGOs resolved that the network would be their self-governing body (much like the interim council the legislation provided for) and would come up with an alternative act and attendant regulations as well as a code of conduct. The NGOs, however, reiterated their commitment to a diplomatic approach in their lobbying efforts. The NGO Standing Committee communicated to the government the network's outstanding concerns and strong resolutions but also made it clear that it would continue to pursue dialogue and was awaiting a response from the government (see NGOSC 1992g).

However in June 1992, NGOs were once again thrown into panic as the government, without forewarning or response to the latest NGO overtures, published the rules and regulations accompanying the NGO Act. This was yet another sign that the government intended to implement the act without resolving the outstanding NGO concerns. The government's intentions were soon confirmed by an official gazette notice announcing the commencement of the act on June 15, 1992.

The NGOSC was seemingly outpaced by events but was quick to react. In an advertisement in the national dailies, the NGOSC urged all NGOs in the network not to register until they attended the next (sixth) workshop to be held in the first week of July. The NGOSC also invited the permanent secretary in the Office of the President and the attorney general to address NGO representatives at this crucial meeting. In parallel dispatches to all NGOs, the NGOSC reiterated that NGOs should not register and highlighted the dangers of the legislation as it stood, especially the absolute powers of the minister, the lack of recourse to the courts, and the registration requirements that included such personal information as spouses' names.

Although the NGOSC call to boycott registration was presented as "advice to delay" until the July meeting, it was nonetheless a call to boycott. The network had seemingly crossed the threshold to confront the state. On their part, government officials were "surprised" that the NGOSC was "concerned" that they had gone ahead and implemented the act despite outstanding issues (NGOSC 1992a). Apparently, the senior government officials could not relate to this concern over the unilateral and "snap" implementation of the act—the predominant modus operandi in the single-party state. Predictably, and in reaction to the ensuing furor, some government departments that offered services to NGOs (such as the immigration department) referred all matters regarding NGOs to the Office of the President (NGOSC 1992a).

Meanwhile, many NGOs expressed grave concern at the government's latest action and pledged their solidarity with the actions of the NGOSC. Similarly, the fledgling opposition parties were solidly behind the NGOs—an indication of their recognition of the NGOs' role in pressing for more space for civil society associational life. The donor community was equally taken aback by the government's unilateral decision to implement the disputed legislation. This was especially so, since the donors' subcommittee on NGOs had made representations to the government regarding the act and sought to be included in the government-NGO dialogue but had yet to receive a response. Donor agencies and home country embassies of foreign NGOs called in their NGO leaders for consultations. For instance, the British high commissioner convened a meeting of ten major British NGOs to consult with them about the situation. Similarly, U.S. and Canadian NGOs and donors such as the UNDP met for similar consultations (NGOSC 1992b; NGOSC 1992f).

In the July meeting, the sixth national workshop, the NGOSC presented a draft of its own legislation, the Private Voluntary Organizations (PVO) Act, as an alternative to the NGO Act. This was unanimously adopted by the network for presentation to the government as the basis for future dialogue (NGOSC 1992h). Neither the permanent secretary in the president's office nor the attorney general attended this meeting to which they had been invited to explain the government's stand. The attorney general, however, indicated that he would be willing to meet with the Standing Committee at a later date. The network resolved to restart the stalled dialogue but called on the government to suspend registration for three months to give the new negotiations a chance. Meanwhile, all NGOs were requested not to register until further notice from the network.

At the same time, there were several undercurrents to enlist the local missions of major donor countries to pressure or lobby the government to reverse its implementation of the act. The actions suggested to the NGOSC included (1) requesting the ambassadors of Britain, the United States, Germany, Japan, and the European Commission, as well as representatives of multilateral bodies, to ask President Moi to reverse the government's decision; (2) encouraging those NGO leaders with personal access to the attorney general to "advise" him that aid to Kenya would be frozen if the act was implemented; and 3) informing the government that if the situation had not improved by September 1992, NGO leaders would publicly announce a freeze on new projects in Kenya and request their home (or donor) governments to withhold aid until the government reversed its decision (Meegan 1992; NGOSC 1992b). Although none of these "hard" tactics was ever employed, they were considered important possibilities to fall back on if the stalemate continued.

The NGOSC sought and received an audience with the attorney general and presented him with its PVO Act in August 1992. He made it clear that the government would not reverse its decision and that all NGOs were required to comply with the law as it stood and register immediately, as there would be no extension in the registration period. The attorney general did, however, look into the NGOs' greatest outstanding concern: that the minister in charge had absolute powers and that NGOs had no recourse to the courts. He agreed to advise the government to provide for appeals to the High Court and to place the administration of the act under a ministry other than the Ministry of State or Office of the President (NGOSC 1992c).

These latest consultations bore fruit as the attorney general tabled and parliament passed amendments to the act in late August 1992. The most important amendment provided for recourse to the High Court as the final arbiter of disputes between NGOs and the minister or the board. Furthermore, the NGO membership on the Board was raised from five to seven, representing one-third of the maximum number of members. (This would give NGOs greater voice on the NGO Board but little possibility of a majority, since most of the other members would be senior government functionaries and it was not yet established whether decisions would be by simple or extraordinary majority.) Although the act would still be administered by the Office of the President, the attorney general stressed that the government had made these new changes in good faith and left the door open for further consultation and action in the future.

Given these positive developments, the NGOSC reconvened the network for a seventh national workshop in October 1992 to reappraise the situation and especially to reconsider whether to register or to continue the boycott and whether, having resolved the most contentious issues, they should cease to lobby. On the question of registration, most members agreed that the most pressing issues had been resolved and they could now go ahead and register. (Indeed, they had obtained favorable amendments on five crucial issues.) However, there were still more issues that needed to be pursued, including the less contentious ones. For instance, the regulations accompanying the act still needed to be reviewed, since NGOs had not contributed to their formulation. (The network had boycotted participation in their formulation after the government passed the minimal amendments in late 1991.) More important, the NGOs did not want to stop here; they still objected to the legislation and sought to have it repealed altogether. This, they asserted, was their ultimate goal and should be pursued tirelessly. In the meantime, as much reform as possible on the existing legislation should be sought (NGOSC 1992i).

By the end of 1992, the government had made good on its promise to respond to more of the NGOs' concerns and had revised the subsidiary legislation, including the published forms. For instance, the more objectionable requirements for personal information from the head officers of NGOs (such as spouses' names) were dropped. Also, where detailed annual budgets and sources of funding were required, estimates were acceptable. To be sure, there were many outstanding issues and concerns, but the NGOSC was satisfied with the changes instituted so far and with the government's renewed spirit of cooperation. Indeed, at the eighth national workshop held in January 1993, the NGOSC—eager to portray its own spirit of goodwill—advised network members to register with the NGO Bureau. The NGOSC started to direct its concerns about administrative aspects of the legislation to the now operational NGO Bureau: for instance, the network's request for an extension of the registration deadline from December 1992 to March 1993 and for the continued recognition of the NGO

Network as the interim council until the NGO Council was constituted (both were granted). These moves by NGOs suggested their
pragmatic acceptance of the NGO Bureau as a legitimate though still
problematic body that they could work with.

Factors Contributing to NGO Success

The first important factor contributing to the success of the NGO challenge to the state was the availability of *political opportunity* to voice
dissent and to pursue oppositional action. This political opportunity
included institutional openings allowing access to the state to express
disagreement with policy and to lobby for changes. For instance, at
the national level, the government had previously responded to
mounting criticism of its single-party rule by setting up a commission
(the KANU Review Committee) in 1990 to solicit public views about
national politics and to reexamine the viability of the single-party
apparatus. In the specific case of the NGO challenge, prevailing
political openings meant that NGO leaders had easier access to the
powerful Office of the President and the office of the attorney general.
Such openings—and state vulnerability—were unlikely before 1990,
when the single-party KANU was the unchallenged power over state
and society. The "expanding structure of political opportunities"
(Tarrow 1991, 13) presented by a state besieged by civil unrest,
nascent opposition parties, and international donors demanding political pluralism allowed NGOs to organize effectively and coordinate
their resources to oppose the threatening legislation.

The second factor that helped the success of this civil society challenge to the state was the level of NGO *collective organization* and
their *combined resources.* In particular, the formation of the NGO
Network and the elected NGO Standing Committee gave NGOs a
strong collective voice. Among the organizational strengths displayed
by the network was the establishment of a functioning secretariat to
coordinate the campaign against the legislation and its adaptability,
as seen in the expansion and specialization of the NGOSC. The work
of the three specialized subcommittees (lobbying, public education,
rules and regulations) was impressive and well-coordinated. For
instance, the lobbying subcommittee pursued vigorous face-to-face
consultations with government officials, and the important personalities within it assured the committee direct access to influential government officers with whom many of the larger NGOs had established
relations from previous cooperation in development projects. The

public education subcommittee also launched a media campaign, including commissioned feature articles in the private press, to highlight NGO contributions to development in Kenya.[7] Perhaps the most important aspect of NGO organization beyond the lobbying and public-relations effort was the ability to come up with alternative legislation. The Private Voluntary Organizations Act involved considerable input from members of the Law Society of Kenya who were also members of the NGOSC.

The third factor that proved just as important to the resolution of this tension to the benefit of civil society was the NGO *alliance with international donor agencies.* International donors consistently facilitated the NGO effort to fight the controlling legislation in various ways. For instance, the United Nations Development Fund and the Ford Foundation in Nairobi funded the initial seminar organized by the Institute for Development Studies of the University of Nairobi. It was at this seminar that NGOs resolved to challenge the legislation instead of adjusting to it. International aid donors also voiced strong support for NGOs, for instance, in memoranda to the NGO Network and in one specific case when the collective donor community issued an official public statement in support of the NGO campaign against the legislation. Finally, an anonymous donor gave funds to establish a fully functional secretariat to coordinate the NGO campaign against the legislation and to supplement funds contributed by each member of the network.

Finally, *NGO alliance with other oppositional forces in civil society* was equally important in the effort to challenge the KANU government. Importantly, the newly legalized opposition parties embraced the NGOs' cause as a contributory part of the broader objective of democratizing the state. At the time, Kenya was preparing to hold its first multiparty general elections since independence, and the newly legalized opposition parties were eager to align with other groups that were opposing the former single party. Moreover, some of the leaders in the NGO Network, such as representatives of the NCCK and the Law Society of Kenya (which was instrumental in creating the PVO Act) were also in the ranks of leading multiparty advocates and opposition party activists. The result of the NGO alliance with the opposition parties was most clearly evident in the electoral platforms of major opposition parties. For instance, in a joint blueprint for postelection action, the major opposition parties undertook to repeal the government's NGO Coordination Act and replace it with the NGO Network's alternative legislation, the Private Voluntary Organizations Act. Incidentally, the publication of this joint blueprint was funded by an international NGO.

One specific incident mentioned above especially highlights the convergence of these four factors in facilitating challenging actions by civil society in Kenya. When the Kenyan government attempted to implement the NGO legislation in mid-1992 without responding to NGO concerns, the NGO Network immediately placed advertisements in national dailies urging all NGOs countrywide to boycott registration and threatening to shut down operations. International donors and opposition parties strongly condemned the government's unilateral action and supported the NGOs' boycott. As a result, because no NGO would register and because the government could not shut down all NGOs (given the potential development shutdown), it was forced to delay the implementation of the law and negotiate further amendments with NGOs—leading to less threatening legislation.

NGOs and the Civil Society Thesis

The case of the community of NGOs in Kenya illustrates the tension and opposition between state and society, as suggested in the literature on civil society in Africa. In addition, it suggests that NGOs were able to force the government to adjust its control over them because of their enhanced leverage due to collective organization and resources, alliances with donors and oppositional forces and crucial access to the state as a result of the prevailing political opportunity. Although this case underscores the thesis that civil society organizations are essential contributors to the democratization movement, it also suggests some limitations.

First, the above explanatory factors (political opportunity, organization and resources, and alliances) are largely external to NGOs. For example, the increase in development resources and donor support that enhanced NGO leverage vis-à-vis the state suggests a substantial involvement of external actors and factors in enabling civil society's triumph over the state. Second, there is no evidence to indicate that the NGOs' oppositional actions were moved by grassroots sentiment; this episode was essentially an organizational effort to secure an enabling environment for NGOs. Indeed, the fact that NGOs in Kenya had traditionally deferred to state control and mounted oppositional action only after their own existence had been threatened *and* after the wave of general societal mobilization was already under way suggests that NGOs are not inherently opposed to a repressive state. Instead, NGOs, with little direct grassroots support, took advantage of an evolving political opportunity to safeguard their existence; only later did they join forces with those organizations that were primarily concerned with broader political changes (newly legalized opposition parties and pressure groups). Even then, NGOs did not see their actions as enhancing democratization; instead, they saw the openings achieved by the democratization movement as giving them a right to operate freely in their development activities.[8] On their part, the newly legalized political parties saw the NGO cause as contributing to the onslaught to force the former single-party state to reform. The opposition parties needed all the resourceful allies they could muster for the task of forcing the KANU government to commit itself to a more democratic and pluralistic political process.

These limitations do not necessarily undermine the fact that NGOs were successful in checking the state's drive for dominance and contributed to the broader movement to ensure an unfettered civil society—which is crucial to an emergent democracy. In the next two chapters, I disaggregate civil society into two individual NGOs to examine two questions: Is this collective behavior replicated by individual NGOs under similar conditions? What actions did individual NGOs take to enhance the democratization movement? The following case studies on the Undugu Society of Kenya and the Green Belt Movement show how these NGOs responded differently to the expanded political opportunity and enhanced resources within the context of democratic change in Kenya. Herein lies the seed of the critique of the civil society thesis: the two faces of civil society.

Notes

1. Indeed, the constitutional amendment that established the de jure single-party state in 1982 was similarly passed within a matter of days.
2. The NCCK is closely tied to the World Council of Churches (WCC), which is committed to the political work of member umbrella organizations. Indeed, the former NCCK secretary general and a most outspoken critic of the Moi government was appointed to head a mission at the WCC in 1993.
3. For instance, the constitutional change in 1982 that turned Kenya into a de jure one-party state was prompted by efforts to register an opposition party by the late Oginga Odinga (later the leader of one of the main opposition parties).
4. But the loud condemnation that each NGO endured in the aftermath and the vilification that the rest were subjected to were testament to the government's willingness to shut down any "errant" organization if possible.
5. In addition to primary sources and daily newspaper reports cited, various issues of the *Weekly Review* documented parts of this NGO-state confrontation. See, for example, *Weekly Review,* June 19, 1992, pp. 24–25;

June 26, 1992, editorial and pp. 28–30; July 17, 1992, pp. 31–32; October 2, 1992, pp. 26–27; and November 6, 1992, p. 32.

6. Attorney General Amos Wako had just recently been appointed. Internationally regarded as a human rights lawyer and with close connections in the NGO community (for instance, he sits on the Undugu Society's governing board), he was thought to be more progressive than the rest of the political establishment. However, his subsequent actions or inaction dulled this initial luster.

7. See *Weekly Review,* May 17, 1991, pp. 29–34; April 3, 1992, pp. 23–30; and August 21, 1992, pp. 27–31.

8. For instance, see the arguments put forth by the NGO Network when the Kenyan government made only a few amendments in the NGO Act in December 1991 against the background of the constitutional change legalizing opposition parties.

4

The Undugu Society
of Kenya

THE UNDUGU SOCIETY OF KENYA projects an image of the conscience of a nation caught in the throes of urban poverty and rapid urbanization. The assuming heights of government office blocks and of the bustling central business district hide the shame of the Nairobi's slums, where over half of the city's 2.5 million residents live. In alleys at the feet of downtown office blocks is the ominous presence of the Nairobi street children who have fled the slum conditions. Undugu seeks to *sensitize* the wider community to the abject poverty of many urban dwellers, to intervene in selective areas in order to *demonstrate* possible solutions, and to *stimulate* other actors in society—in particular, the government—toward greater intervention. Most Kenyans readily associate the Undugu Society of Kenya with street children. They were Undugu's initial concern, and one that eventually led to the NGO's greater involvement in the slum communities in Nairobi. Today, Undugu is one of the largest indigenous NGOs and a prominent actor in the NGO sector in Kenya.

In this chapter, I offer a historical discussion of the Undugu Society, highlighting its growth, work philosophy, and activities involving the urban underprivileged population. Then I present a descriptive account of my field experience with Undugu, focusing on one ongoing integrated development program in a slum community in the eastern part of Nairobi. This section also discusses my field findings within the parameters of the civil society–democratization argument. I am especially interested in exploring the extent to which the NGO, through its community development programs, has contributed to the mobilization of the slum communities and, in particular, to a change in their political capacities.

Undugu's contribution to democratization efforts in Kenya is less explicit than the collective NGO efforts discussed in Chapter 3. Undugu does not appear to have engaged the Kenyan state as the

NGO Network did, even though its director (Ezra Mbogori) was a leading actor in the NGO Network. But neither has the Undugu disengaged or exited from relations with the state; to the contrary, it has continued to work closely with the Kenyan government in development efforts. The case of Undugu contradicts present theoretical understanding—demonstrated in Chapter 3—that civil society organizations are necessarily at the forefront of challenging the repressive state in Africa. It suggests that certain actors in civil society do not seek to oppose the repressive state but instead seek accommodation with it. The Undugu case reveals an organization that is progressive in its working philosophy, that moves its grassroots clients to mount challenging actions when opportunities arise, but that is itself immobile when presented with opportunities to enhance the actions of its clients or other actors opposing the state.

Why does Undugu not engage the state despite the prevailing political opportunity, its resources, its grassroots mobilization, and the presence of obvious conflicts that it can legitimately pursue? In spite of its indifference to opportunities to challenge the Kenyan state to reform, can Undugu still contribute to the democratic ferment in Kenya? For instance, do the organization's development activities enhance the capacity of its clients to engage in challenges to the repressive state?

History and Institutional Growth[1]

What is today a large and well-institutionalized NGO started as a one-man initiative for street children in Nairobi in 1973. A Dutch Catholic priest, Father Arnold Grol, started the program that would later blossom into the Undugu Society of Kenya. In 1972, he arrived from Tanzania for his first urban apostolate. Posted at St. Teresa's Catholic Church in Eastleigh—a poor, densely populated village that borders the sprawling Mathare Valley slum—Father Grol was charged with ministering to the local youth. He immediately noticed that most of the youth in this area did not attend school, had no meaningful occupation, and were left to idle in the slums. Some of them, mostly between the ages of eight and fifteen years, had descended on the city streets and established their "homes" as street children. This latter group—to which those still in the slums eventually graduated—had earned the name "parking boys" from their primary occupation of guiding motorists to vacant parking bays and guarding their vehicles for a few coins. Besides this, they were also involved in petty thievery and their trademark pastime of sniffing gasoline or glue to get high.

In 1973, Grol established recreational youth clubs in three Nairobi slums (Makadara, Kariobangi, and Mathare), where most of the street children came from. Grol also sought to establish an "open house" in the city where these street children could go for shelter, a shower, and a meal. This was established at the St. Paul's Chaplaincy of the University of Nairobi, and other churches and the Red Cross donated meals. The reception center also provided street children with a safe haven from the numerous police sweeps they were subjected to, mostly in cleanup campaigns in anticipation of international events in the city. Grol's undertaking was an important step in establishing a rapport with the street children that has lasted to this day and has endowed Undugu with legitimacy as a helper in the children's eyes. Many of these children expressed a desire for education, which was in stark contrast to the general view of the public and the media that they were hardened delinquents beyond rehabilitation. In reality, most of them were from very poor families, often single-parent homes in the slums; most had some schooling but had had to drop out because of the lack of school fees or uniforms or other basic needs, such as food. They were often forced into the streets to fend for themselves (Grol 1992, n.d.; Cowley 1987).

In 1975, the youth clubs that Grol had started in the slums were registered as the Undugu Youth Centers. A variety of activities were already being conducted by then. Apart from recreational activities, these clubs were providing basic education in a nonformal setting for street and slum children. In 1978, the Undugu Society of Kenya was formally registered as an NGO under the Societies Act, with the primary goal of finding solutions to the street-children problem in Nairobi. By this time, Undugu had become aware that the street-children phenomenon was a symptom of a larger problem resident in the slum communities these children came from. Undugu therefore sought to move from its sole focus on street children to the fathers and mothers in the slum communities (Kibe n.d.; Mbogori 1992, 9). Since the NGO could not service all slum areas in Nairobi, and in keeping with an evolving *experimenter-stimulator* objective, it chose to concentrate on the three slums of Mathare, Pumwani, and Kibera.

Over the years, Undugu has grown from a simple one-man initiative seeking to ease the suffering of Nairobi street children to a well-institutionalized national NGO intervening in a number of slum areas in Nairobi. Today, Undugu has over twenty different program activities in several areas (Kibera, Mathare, Pumwani, Eastleigh, and Kariobangi in Nairobi, and Katangi in Machakos district). Undugu also has a professional staff of over 140 (mostly social workers, but also business advisors and community nurses) and has established field offices in three city slum communities (Mathare, Pumwani, and Kibera) and in one semiarid area outside Nairobi (USK 1989).

In its program activities, Undugu has remained faithful to its primary goal of finding solutions to the street-children problem. Most of its activities are in this area or are linked to this central concern. Over the years, Undugu has also evolved an integrated approach to community development that includes community organization, income-generating activities, community health, and shelter improvement (see Appendix A). Along with this programmatic expansion, Undugu has experienced tremendous expansion in its budgetary outlays. Available figures show a precipitous growth in income: for instance, in 1991, total income stood at 42 million Kenyan Shillings (K Sh) (US$1.4 million), up from K Sh 16 million (US$500,000) in 1986 and less than K Sh 2 million (US$67,000) in 1981 (USK 1989, 1990a, 1992, Buiys 1984).[2] (See Table 4.1.)

According to my own calculations based on the latest available figures (USK 1989), 70 percent of the expenditure goes directly to program activities, and the remainder is used for administrative support. Of greater interest is the fact that Undugu generates between 35 and 60 percent of its overall income through its own commercial production units, such as the motor mechanics unit, which offers vehicle services, or the business development unit, which provides consultancy services on a commercial basis. This internally generated income is sufficient to cover Undugu's administrative costs. The rest is received mainly from foundations in Germany and Holland, various sources in the United States, and Undugu's own fund-raising initiative through the Undugu Friends Circles in different countries, including Kenya.

Undugu's achievements are difficult to quantify, but the institutional growth evident over the last twenty years, the range of activities carried out, and the number of communities served are indicators of its impact. In terms of numbers, Undugu is involved in three integrated community development programs in three slum areas in Nairobi serving over 40,000 people. It has also aided in the improvement of slum conditions by helping residents construct over 1,000 low-cost but durable shelters, improving sanitation services, and helping business ventures in the slums. Undugu has also benefited thousands of street children by providing either rehabilitation or temporary care services, such as access to medical attention. Available figures reveal only a fraction of the work Undugu has done with street children and potential street children in slum communities over the last two decades. For instance, each year, 700 slum and street children go through the informal Undugu Basic Education Program (UBEP); another 300-plus children are given fee scholarships for reg-

Table 4.1 Undugu's Total and Internally Generated Income, 1986–91

Year	Total Income (TI)		Internal Revenue (IR)		IR as % of TI
	K Sh Million	(US$ Million)	K Sh Million	(US$ Million)	
1986	15.8	(0.5)	9.4	(0.3)	59.4
1987	20.0	(0.7)	10.5	(0.35)	53.5
1988	19.0	(0.6)	10.0	(0.3)	52.6
1989	23.8	(0.8)	9.4	(0.3)	39.5
1990	21.7	(0.7)	13.1	(0.4)	60.3
1991	42.2	(1.4)	15.3	(0.5)	36.2

Source: Compiled by the author from USK financial and annual reports, 1986–91.

ular schools, and 60 to 70 youths are trained in informal-sector apprenticeships (USK 1989, 1992).

Undugu's growth over the last two decades has been demonstrated further by steps toward institutionalization. Following an evaluation of Undugu's organizational structure in 1986, a number of changes were made to streamline its operations. The daily operations of the NGO were entrusted to an executive director, and a board of directors and a board of trustees would be in charge of the overall programmatic directions. Grol was elected the chairperson of both boards, and Fabio Dallape, Grol's successor, joined as a member of the board of directors after relinquishing the executive director position, thus providing continuity. The board of directors and the board of trustees include leading national personalities, such as current attorney general Amos Wako, the secretary-general of the National Council of Churches of Kenya, and a judge of the High Court (see Appendix A). Moreover, a clear hierarchy and organizational structure, as well as many bureaucratic procedures, have emerged as indispensable aspects of Undugu's daily activities. Undugu's institutional growth is also prominently underlined by its ubiquitous headquarters—a green and white three-story building overlooking the Majengo-Pumwani area and within earshot of the perpetual din of its informal-sector district.

Undugu's institutionalization, however, is a development that the NGO had guarded against because of the fear of distancing itself from its clients. Undugu's founder expressed his misgivings thus:

Many institutions and organizations are not interested in helping the marginalized people. These organizations have rigid rules, timetables,

and demand that certain procedures be followed before they can be of
help. Undugu is different. We must not be an institution or aim to be
one. We must stick to our target groups, the poor and the neglected. We
do not want to be as big as possible. (Grol in Kibe n.d., 3)

Similarly, a former executive director exhorts Undugu's adaptability
to change but shuns institutionalization as a course for fulfilling its
original goals:

Undugu should remain as open to changes and as flexible as possible.
Except in very few areas like accounting and to some extent UBDU
[Undugu Business Development Unit] it should avoid as much as
possible acquiring institutional and/or bureaucratic characteristics.
(Dallape in Kibe n.d., 5).

As my fieldwork experience revealed, however, Undugu as an NGO
is thoroughly institutionalized and has a well-developed bureaucratic
structure. Developments over the last twenty years, and especially the
last decade, exude its institutional trappings. Bureaucratic procedures
are evident in many areas, including service provision (for example,
school fee sponsorship, intervention toward street children's rehabilitation) and much of the in-house decision making. Despite Grol's initial misgivings, Undugu does "demand that certain procedures be
followed before [it] can be of help." It would be a mistake to view this
institutionalization and bureaucratization as having alienated Undugu
from its target group, however, since most of these procedures are in
place primarily for ensuring accountability. As director, Mbogori
viewed this institutionalization as a necessary and desirable step in
Undugu's growth (see Grol and Mbogori in Kibe n.d.; USK 1980).

Undugu's institutionalization or bureaucratization has not been
without a cost. This development has short-circuited Undugu's philosophy of moving its target groups to actions that undermine the
fundamental causes of their poverty. This is suggestive of what Piven
and Cloward (1977) regard as the conservatism that emerges in (radical) movement organizations as they become institutionalized and,
more importantly, as they are transformed into bureaucratic organizations coacting with government bureaucracies. In the Undugu case,
this conservatism (in terms of a lack of organizational participation in
the democratic movement) can be partially attributed to its amicable
relations with the Kenyan government and its bureaucracies. This is
especially evident where Undugu has distanced itself from undertaking or facilitating community actions that are logical conclusions of
its own philosophy but may be "political" or appear to constitute
direct challenges to the state.

Undugu's Working Philosophy

Undugu recognizes that the slum community is constrained by "a multiplicity of problems: economic, health, social, education" (USK n.d.e, 3). In this environment, Undugu believes in "helping a community help itself, not charity" (USK [1986a], 1989). In particular, Undugu emphasizes interventions that address social problems with programs that recognize the *economic* roots of such problems and thus seek to not only alleviate these social problems but also impact the economic fortunes of communities or individuals. Moreover, Undugu focuses on the individual as the appropriate entry point for helping a community; the goal is to make that individual self-reliant and conscious of his or her community. It is through the individual and for the individual that the community can be developed (USK n.d.e). More importantly, Undugu views itself not as the panacea for the problems of urban poverty in Kenya but as a small experimenter whose solutions can stimulate others (including NGOs and the government) and can be adapted to other communities (Grol n.d.; USK 1989, 1990a, 1992, USK n.d.e). Therefore, Undugu does not seek to provide a total solution to all underdevelopment in all slum communities but to influence other actors by example (Mbogori 1992). These ideals are reflected in the overall aims articulated by Undugu:

1. To enhance the socioeconomic status of people in low-income areas through an integrated approach to community development and small-scale business development;

2. To enhance the responsibility and capacity of the people in low-income areas for their own development;

3. To provide nonfinancial assistance to other institutions that are involved in similar activities; and

4. To progressively reduce dependency on donor funding through Undugu's own income-generating initiatives (USK [1986a], n.d.e).

The problems that define slum conditions and that Undugu encounters in its work in these communities include a lack of community organization and mobilization and a general apathy toward community development; acute unemployment, inadequate or poor shelter, and poor health information and facilities (USK 1989, 1990a,

1992, n.d.e). In response to these situations, Undugu has evolved four core departments that make up its slum community intervention strategy: the Community Organization Department, the Business Development Unit, the Low-Cost Shelter Department, and the Community Health Department.

The Community Organization Department (COD) is the most crucial unit, especially in the early phases of a program. COD staff typically interact with community members on a daily basis to define community problems and work out strategies for action. COD works through established community organizations (such as women's groups organized around an economic activity) and considers this the best way to gain a foothold in the community and to facilitate future cooperation. COD social workers seek to strengthen the community organization network by offering leadership training to members of such groups (USK n.d.c). From the existing groups and others whose establishment the COD facilitates, Undugu is able to achieve community participation in its development programs:

> Staff and beneficiaries play a big role in the identification of their community needs. The beneficiaries will usually put forward their issues. USK staff comes in and facilitates deeper insight into the origins of their problems and into the best ways of approaching them in an integrated way. Staff make use of existing social structures and are not regarded as intruders. (USK [1986a])

Community participation is an expressive and much exhorted goal in Undugu's project activities and is a clearly evident achievement, as witnessed in my fieldwork. "In Undugu we work *with* the people not for the people. . . . People only feel themselves responsible when, by discussing with them together, we look for solutions to difficulties they bring forward themselves" (Grol in Kibe, n.d., 9). The focus on the individual is especially pervasive in project activities and is perhaps expressed best by the Community Organization Department's own perspective: "COD seeks to work with and through people. We never accomplish things for people as we believe that people, whatever their condition and station in life, have an inherent capacity to improve their own condition for better. Doing things for people denies them humanity and responsibility" (USK n.d.a).

Undugu views itself as supplementing rather than doing the work of the government and, as such, maintains amicable relations with central and local government authorities. In many instances, Undugu's work has been facilitated by cooperation with local administration officials or with central government agencies. Little of Undugu's work has been viewed as challenging the political status quo or existing government programs. The organization has eschewed confrontation with the administration and has instead pursued activities that are noncontroversial. For example, Undugu helped one slum community construct improved low-cost shelter on government land that the community had explicitly been permitted to occupy by the authorities. At the same time, Undugu persistently declined to do the same for an adjacent community that continues to live in paper "igloos" on undeveloped private land. This is essentially because assisting the latter community would be abetting the illegal act of "squatting," which could result in conflicts with the government.

Is Undugu's apparent lack of political commitment to assist seemingly powerless groups a reflection of what Fowler (1991b) sees as the gap between NGO modernization projects and empowerment? Indeed, as I argue later, Undugu's unwillingness to engage in politically sensitive pursuits is a serious limitation to its work in the slums and its contributions to pluralizing civil society. However, this lack of will "to go the extra mile" does not stem from a lack of institutional understanding of the political dynamics that keep the poor impoverished in the slums. Indeed, a past executive director asserts that "the solution to squatters has to be on a political level" (Dallape n.d., 3). Dallape, who is a trained social scientist, offers the following insightful analysis of the political dynamics that keep the slum populations marginalized:

> The reason why situations of social injustice exist is that parts of the populations continue to bear these injustices humbly and passively. In most cases this is because they need the assistance of those who are in positions of power. The more people overcome their dependency, the more they are able to make use of their capacities. Instead, for instance, of people choosing leaders just because they had been bribed with kilos of sugar, they should choose leaders on the basis of merit. Only in this will people demand certain standards of their leaders. If people depend less on those in power, they are able to negotiate better with them: from positions of equality. (Dallape in Kibe n.d., 9–10)

Bolder critiques of the life conditions in the slum communities and calls for more "political" solutions were evident from interviews and interactions with Undugu's field-workers and especially community members. However, as an organization, Undugu does not subscribe to overt political actions, much less to expressly politicizing slum communities toward solving their problems. Indeed, Undugu is at pains to distance itself from any implication of the inevitable politicization of slum communities through its development work. As Ezra Mbogori, then current director, explained:

> I'd like to think what we do is actually sensitizing. I am being particu-
> larly careful about using words like "awareness," "conscientization"
> because of their controversial nature. They are received as confronta-
> tional and as inciting communities. This is not what we do. What we
> do is work with communities in a manner that would develop their
> own understanding of the realities around them, and develop an ability
> to deal with those realities. That is the same as sensitizing them.
> (Mbogori in Kibe n.d., 20)

Does this distancing from active politics preclude organizations
like Undugu from contributing to the democratic ferment in Kenya?
Perhaps not. It is important to recall the influence of the broader
political context on NGO actions as established in chapters 2 and 3.
More specifically, the reluctance on the part of Undugu to engage in
overt political actions reflects organizational stasis stemming from
the political context it has operated and matured in. This is particularly true when we consider that it was in the 1980s that Undugu
shifted from curative to preventive approaches to urban poverty
issues (USK [1986a]; Grol n.d.).[3] One would expect this shift to lead
to more politically sensitive solutions targeted at the underlying
causes of urban poverty, such as lack of land tenure in slum communities or periodic and indiscriminate demolitions of slum villages.
However, during the 1980s, the Moi government was most inhos-
pitable to independent actions in civil society as it moved to consolidate state power, culminating in the legalization of the single-party
state in 1982. Thereafter, the Moi regime continued in its efforts to
undermine existing civil society institutions, such as through the
annexation of *Maendeleo ya Wanawake* and COTU (the national
women's and trade union movements, respectively) into the party-
state machinery. Further efforts to subdue other organizations such as
the cooperative movement, local self-help groups, church bodies, and
NGOs are well documented (see Throup 1987; Widner 1992;
Kanyinga 1993; Ngethe and Odero 1992).

In this context, then, there was little latitude for radical political
action by NGOs.[4] Annelis Leemans (1982), who studied Undugu's
approaches to community development during the transition from
curative to preventive approaches, underscores these contextual limitations during the period of study (1976–80):

> The present politico-economic Kenyan context dictates the upper and
> lower limits for a movement like Undugu to rouse the poor to commu-
> nal action. The politically accepted improvement approach does leave
> little room for organized pressure group activities, communal disobedi-
> ence as expressed in strikes and demonstrations against social injustice

or unacceptable economic structures. . . . Movements and trends like Harambee, Nation Building and the call for Nyayo are the politically sublimated and legitimated desirables. Voluntary and other organizations find in them the social base to operate and mobilize the poor towards participation in nation building and self reliant development. (Leemans 1982, 24)

Leemans's observations are suggestive of the extent to which even mundane "modernization" projects are conditioned by the prevailing political opportunities. Indeed, the subservience of development organizations to the state and its ideology was pervasive in the social development scene in Kenya until the dawn of multiparty politics in 1990-92, when overt challenges to the existing political order were possible. And yet, even with the expanded opportunity during the transition to a multiparty electoral system, Undugu's reactions were subdued. As recent as 1992, when many civil society institutions, including other NGOs, were at the forefront of challenging the overbearing but crumbling former single-party state, Undugu remained politically diminutive and preferred not to "rock the boat." This projected image as an apolitical organization was well expressed in private communication prior to my fieldwork:

[Regarding] our role in conscientization and/or leadership development it is important to state at the outset that we have to be careful about the image that exists out there, particularly in Government about us. The view that we are a well meaning, benign, apolitical children's agency suits us very well. (Ezra Mbogori letter to the author 1992)

This projected image was confirmed by my interactions with NGO officials during my field activities. Undugu's adherence to this apolitical stance is indeed perplexing, not only because its working philosophy highlights empowerment but also because its director, Ezra Mbogori, was among the leaders (if not *the* leader) of the NGO Network that was so successful in opposing the NGO Coordination Act (see Chapter 3). Both Undugu's working philosophy and, given the immense influence that NGO heads have on "their" NGOs, Mbogori's actions within the NGO Network suggest that Undugu is conscious of empowerment possibilities. Yet the organization does not explicitly further these goals through its projects, even as opportunities arise to do so. Undugu's limited *organizational* ability to respond to the available political opportunities is impeded by its bureaucratization and, most importantly, by its close contacts (some would say cozy relations) with the state and establishment elites (see particularly the composition of its boards [Appendix A]).

Undugu's success in its work in Nairobi's slums is based primarily on its active involvement in the communities it serves and on encouraging community organization and grassroots participation in its programs. Most importantly, its interventions have largely been successful because of the integrated approach it emphasizes in dealing with community problems. In particular, the centrality of economic components of most interventions (such as income-generating and savings activities) in response to the underlying economic causes of social problems has proved to be very effective (USK n.d.e). Indeed, in the course of its involvement in development work, Undugu has discovered that programs that focus only on the manifest social aspects of a community's problems and ignore the underlying economic concerns have little impact in alleviating the community's condition (USK [1986a], 10). Although this *socioeconomic* approach has a lot to commend it and has produced impressive results in Undugu's work, without overt challenges to the *sociopolitical* arrangements that continue to impoverish the urban poor, the NGO's actions may be of limited help in solving the plight of slum dwellers in Kenya.

The next section highlights opportunities for more overtly political actions that Undugu could undertake or facilitate in its projects. Conversely, it points out Undugu's limitations in altering the fundamental life conditions of the urban poor.

Institutional and Grassroots Opportunities for Political Action

As an organization working in slum communities, Undugu occupies the middle ground between the underrepresented slum dwellers and the government. This suggests that Undugu may be in a position to transmit the preferences of slum dwellers to the government. But as is evident in this chapter, Undugu has not attempted to do so—although it has encouraged its client communities to do so themselves. Undugu has seemingly been more concerned with carrying out its development projects than in engaging the state over issues touching on the interests of its client communities. Undugu has similarly kept its distance from agitation by some of its beneficiaries, even though such agitation has evolved from its own efforts at enhancing their capacity for action through community organization or income-generating activities.

There is a distinct difference between how Undugu as an *organization* has responded to opportunities for institutional political action that would have contributed to the pressure on the Kenyan state to reform and how its grassroots clients have responded to similar opportunities. The experience of the Undugu Society of Kenya elaborated below suggests that not all civil society organizations engage the state, notwithstanding available opportunities and resources. The fact that Undugu's indifference to its potential contribution to the broader democratization effort occurred even as some of its beneficiaries engaged the state raises serious doubts as to whether civil society organizations actually transmit grassroots preferences or act on their own independent preferences. This has obvious implications for the view that civil society organizations may be democracy-enhancing institutions. It also suggests that there may be other factors (other than political opportunity, organization and resources, and alliances) that impinge on the ability or willingness of societal organizations to pursue oppositional actions against a repressive state.

Kitui Village: A History of an Urban Squatter Settlement[5]

The Kitui-Pumwani Program (KPP) is one of Undugu's most successful integrated development programs. The program serves a three-village slum community—Kitui, Kanuku, and Kinyago—situated in the Majengo-Pumwani area of the eastlands of Nairobi. The Majengo-Pumwani area is one of the most densely populated in Nairobi. Much of the area consists of traditional Swahili-type mud and wattle, tin-roofed houses (thus the name *majengo*) and run-down tenements of stone built in the colonial era. It stretches to the Eastleigh neighborhood that used to be the segregated Asian quarter. Most of the residents live in poverty, but the situation is worse in the three villages that make up the KPP area. Prior to Undugu's intervention, the most evident manifestation of this poverty was the housing condition.

Kitui village was previously known as "igloo city" because of the shape of the shelters that the residents made from paper, polyethylene, and sticks. Kitui village was first settled by three women from Kitui district (including Mama Ngusie, whom I interviewed) who were given permission by local KANU officials to build temporary structures in the area in October 1966. Within a year, an estimated 120 other squatters had joined the pioneers, and by 1968 the number had risen to 550. By 1969, about 700 people had settled in the village, and a school and a church had been constructed. Thus the residents had established a community and named it *Kitui* after the district most of them hailed from. Although some settlers had built semipermanent mud and wattle houses, most of the residents could afford only to put up paper and polyethylene igloo-like structures (Karobia n.d.).

In June 1970, fire gutted most of the structures while the residents were away attending *Madaraka* (self-government) day celebrations. The residents rebuilt their shelters and resettled, but in November 1972, a different kind of tragedy struck when the Nairobi City Council demolished the entire village to make way for the Eastleigh Air Base (now Moi Air Base). Many of the residents were arrested and repatriated to their rural home areas. However, up to 350 others remained, as they had nowhere else to go. The local member of parliament lobbied the Kenya Air Force commanders to allow the remaining squatters to settle on part of the field that the air force would not be using. This request was granted, and the residents rebuilt their paper houses in 1973 (Karobia n.d.).

This initial demolition was a precursor to an evolving government policy on unplanned settlements in both urban and rural areas (see Mbithi and Barnes 1975). The policy of slum demolition as a measure of controlling unplanned settlements was one that the Kenyan government had adopted from its colonial predecessor. One of the colonial government's largest and most notable demolitions was that of the African settlement in the Mathare Valley slum in 1954 (Pratt 1992). In this action, code-named Operation Anvil, the colonial government destroyed houses and forcefully moved over 20,000 Africans from the slum whom they suspected of supporting the Mau Mau insurgency for independence (see Pratt 1992, 68, citing Amis 1983). The postindependence Kenyan government has pursued a similar policy, although it is couched in less political terms. The predominant justifications offered for periodic slum demolitions have been related to city bylaws (such as sanitary standards), planned development, or law and order—especially where the land is privately owned (*Weekly Review,* June 8, 1990, 15–17).

The 1972 demolition of Kitui village was therefore part of the government's evolving policy of controlling slum settlements. Prior to the Kitui incident, several demolitions involving thousands of individuals had been effected. For example, in 1971, three major demolitions were carried out in two areas: Kaburini, where 8,943 structures were destroyed and 48,000 persons displaced, and two Eastleigh villages, where close to 2,000 structures were destroyed and 20,000 individuals displaced (Pratt 1992). Despite the government's stated policy that no slum settlement should be demolished without an alternative site being provided (Republic of Kenya 1966), normally no such alternative or even fair warning was provided. The initial Kitui demolition was therefore part of a broader undertaking by the government that was set to continue. Usually, the demolitions were carried out at daybreak by city *askaris* (city council inspectors) with bulldozers and trucks, backed by armed police officers. As there was nothing the slum dwellers could do to counter this massive force, most of the demolition operations were scenes of panic and confusion and were met with little resistance from the squatters. After suffering a number of such demolitions, Kitui villagers evolved an innovative preemptive mechanism. Since their shelters were essentially collapsible polyethylene and stick hovels, they would dismantle them before daybreak and hide them and their few belongings in the bushes and proceed with their daily activities. When the demolition squads arrived at dawn, they would find a cleared plot that would turn into a teeming village by evening.

In the early 1980s, the government's policy on slum and squatter settlements seemed to have shifted. The practice of demolishing squatter settlements diminished, and the government allowed improvements to be made in slum communities (USK [1983]). This indicated the government's recognition of the fact that the slum communities were a permanent facet of the urban areas. Other than halting the demolitions, the government was now involved in providing services to some of these communities and allowing NGOs to do so (USK [1983]). Kitui village was one of the slum communities that benefited from this policy shift. The Undugu Society of Kenya had started some programs (such as the UBEP and school fee sponsorship) for Kitui village in 1978. In 1980, the government gave a donation of K Sh 20,000 (approximately US$1,000)[6] toward a nursery school in the village, and the Ministry of Culture and Social Services provided chairs. Moreover, the Nairobi City Council started a mobile children's clinic in the area.

However, despite these interventions, the residents of Kitui village continued to live in squalor and under the constant fear of being evicted by the city council or private landlords or having their homes destroyed by fire. On the night of June 12, 1983, the village was razed by a fire that quickly consumed the paper and polyethylene shelters, leaving the residents destitute and homeless (Karobia n.d.). Apart from the usual emergency assistance that many humanitarian NGOs deliver to such victims, Undugu sought to help the community with a more lasting solution. After consultations with community members, especially village leaders, Undugu established that the residents' most urgent need was more durable houses. This presented a problem: the villagers were squatters on land belonging to the Nairobi City Council, and putting up more durable shelter—more permanent structures—would be illegal. Rebuilding their paper igloos would not be a "sustainable" (permanent) solution. Having ignited community participation in its previous programs and in these consultations,

Undugu offered to help the community with materials and technical assistance if the residents would contribute labor and part of the material costs for the new shelters. In addition, the residents would have to approach the authorities for permission to build more permanent structures on public land.

Undugu had been operating in Kitui village since 1978 and had gained a great deal of legitimacy in the community and had established networks of action. In addition to the UBEP and school sponsorship program, Undugu was already involved in a variety of activities in the village, including community health work, literacy programs, and income-generating schemes for residents—especially women's groups (knitting or sewing items, or selling paraffin, water, or crafts). Moreover, Undugu had facilitated the formation of several groups, including the village committee, which was made up of twelve elected community members who deliberated on community issues. The committee also fulfilled administrative tasks in the village (for example, coordinating weekly village cleanups) and represented the community on various Undugu project committees. It is through these established representative groups, especially the village committee, that Undugu encouraged the community to approach the government for permission to put up more durable shelters and settle on public land. The community took up the challenge.

The tactic of prodding the community to undertake this action was deliberate on the part of Undugu: "mobilizing the people for such a common effort will be a good leadership training for the committee who will bear the whole responsibility of this effort under our guidance" (USK [1983], 2). This tactic was not based on unsound premises: giving the community a chance to organize around a specific interest and to interact with state agents and officialdom in a lobbying capacity was an important step toward empowerment that had begun with the financial independence offered by social-economic projects and the confidence instilled through community organization and leadership training.

The Kitui village committee approached local administrative officials with Undugu's help and, after a number of consultations, was granted permission to rebuild more durable houses—provided they did this on city council land and not on the area reserved for the air base (USK [1983]). Following this, Undugu, with the help of the local administration and the village committee, demarcated the land and organized the villagers to construct 500 mostly one-room mud and wattle houses (USK [1983]). The timing was helpful for the villagers' case: 1983 was an election year following an abortive coup in August 1982 that had shaken Moi's four-year-old regime. In addition, some of the senior politicians in KANU had just been expelled from the party, and early elections had been called, ostensibly to "clean house." The electorate—and especially the Nairobi electorate, of which the slum dwellers were a formidable portion—had to be pacified. The government therefore might have been willing to make concessions to such groups in the hope that this would drum up support for itself.

A second slum village improvement project followed shortly thereafter in the nearby Kanuku village. As in Kitui village, Kanuku villagers had built numerous igloo-type structures made of paper, polyurethane, and sticks. In addition to the threat of eviction, Kanuku residents lived with the danger of seasonal floods from the Nairobi River, which bordered the village. They lived in even more squalid conditions: the settlement had no running water or sanitary facilities, and the residents used a grassy and bushy floodplain between the last row of houses and the riverbank as the "toilet zone"—where, according to one villager, "one would avoid one lump of human waste only to step into the next on his way to deposit his." In the case of Kanuku village, the local chief and other administration officials approached Undugu to help the residents improve their living conditions. As a result, Undugu helped Kanuku villagers build 250 two-roomed houses along the lines of the Kitui pilot project. Because of the lessons learned from the Kitui experience, Undugu was able to better organize the community and to effect a better village design, which included planned infrastructure such as pit latrines, footpaths, and a road (SINA 1986).

The Kinyago village was a new addition to the Kitui and Kanuku area. The residents of Kinyago actually migrated there after being evicted from private land in the neighboring Eastleigh estate. Once again, Undugu was approached by the local administration to help in resettling the squatters alongside the other two villages. The administration officials involved included the local chief, the local district officer, and the Nairobi provincial commissioner, since this move involved the allocation of alternative sites for the evicted squatters (according to the government's policy). Following consultation between the residents and administration officials, Undugu was requested to help them resettle on four acres of land allocated by the city authorities next to Kanuku village. As a result, another 300 two-room houses as well as a community hall and other infrastructure, including latrines and trenches, were built through communal efforts (USK [1986b], [1986c], SINA 1986).

The shelter improvement projects in the three villages are central components of the KPP. A variety of other programs introduced by Undugu have also contributed to improving the life conditions of slum dwellers in Kitui-Pumwani. Among these are various income-generating programs (such as charcoal, paraffin, or water kiosks; arts and crafts women's groups; and brick making), community health programs, and school sponsorships for slum children. The shelter improvement project has provided the communities with security from the frequent fires that destroyed their previous dwellings and a healthier environment (in particular, pit latrines). The involvement of local administration officials at various stages of the shelter improvement projects (authorization to build semipermanent shelters, land demarcation, community organization, and service provision) as well as their continued involvement in many of the ongoing program activities diminishes the danger of eviction. Furthermore, the local administration promised from the very beginning that the communities would not be evicted without the provision of an alternative site.

Despite the general improvement in the welfare of the community, one fundamental problem remains a source of insecurity: land tenure. Indeed, for these communities, land remains the core issue, and they see it as one of the essential prerequisites to permanently elevating themselves out of urban poverty. From selected interviews with community leaders (village elders, elected village committee members, and women's group leaders), it was evident that although they appreciate the improvements brought by Undugu, they still have unfulfilled desires of self-reliance. Community leaders who were interviewed cited rural poverty and lack of land as the foremost factors that made them and other residents flee their home areas and settle in Nairobi. In particular, the early settlers who came to Nairobi in the late 1950s during the Mau Mau independence war had fled their rural reserves as youngsters and cannot trace their homelands. A notable number of women, most of whom head households, were either disinherited or divorced and had to move to the city in search of a livelihood.

Most of the community leaders interviewed asserted that their situation would be greatly improved if they could acquire land—city plots with tenure, where they could build rental houses and their own permanent dwellings, or rural land, where they could individually or collectively start farming activities. The community leaders interviewed are well aware of the fact that there is little likelihood of getting land from the government. First, there is little government land left for resettlement programs such as the postindependence Million-Acres Settlement Scheme. Second, such land allocations have become so politicized that it may be possible to secure a grant only from the highest authorities—that is, the president. Third, the corruption involved in such land grants and in private land-buying schemes is phenomenal; many poor shareholders of land-buying companies or cooperatives have been defrauded by their leaders or political patrons.

On its part, Undugu categorically refuses to engage in the political maneuvers that might lead to such land grants or even to guarantees of tenure for the land the villagers now occupy. Indeed, Undugu's field officials are worried about what will happen once the "goodwill" tenure granted by the city authorities for the Kitui, Kinyago, and Kanuku villages expires. Given the NGO's stated nonpolitical stand and its own history, it is inconceivable that it would vehemently (read politically) oppose moves to clear the area for other developments. However, this may not be the case with the residents. Already, the social and economic programs in the area have instilled in them a sense of community, and their own experiences in working with authorities directly and negotiating the goodwill tenure have given them a good foothold to oppose such a move. Moreover, it may well be that, due to the alleviation of poverty, their greater degree of economic independence has wiped out much of the communal apathy that characterized the pre-1983 period.

Regardless, the community members have proved themselves to be an enterprising lot. For instance, there are various ongoing attempts to acquire agricultural land or city plots by the three villages through member associations. Each village membership organization has communal savings from monthly contributions from individuals and from group projects. The purpose of these savings is to provide money for investments, such as new business ventures, or to purchase agricultural land. The village committees look for the land to be purchased, and Undugu has agreed to facilitate further loans to secure the land as well as to help the community relocate, provide aid in agricultural development, and provide many of the social and economic programs offered now. The success of an Undugu-supported urban agricultural project on the flood-prone area near the riverbank (formerly the "toilet zone") has been a convincing experiment for the residents. These continuing efforts toward acquiring land can be seen as a positive step in community self-organization, which may be a precursor to independent action to fight for their rights—especially if the government decides to evict them (see below).

Undugu's integrated program in the Kitui-Pumwani area has had important social and economic effects on the community. However, the sustained apolitical stance taken by the organization has limited its involvement in enabling the community to transcend its impoverishment. The community seems to want to go further, and it may need Undugu to intercede for it, but the NGO's own institutional character does not allow it. For instance, adjacent to Undugu's field office in Kitui-Pumwani is a surviving igloo village whose residents live in the same unsanitary conditions as the program villages did before Undugu's intervention. In 1992, the village was ravaged by a midnight fire. Shortly thereafter, the villagers approached Undugu for help in rebuilding their shelters in more durable form, as it had in the three program villages. There was a problem, however: the land on which the igloo village stood was private land. Undugu could not help them build permanent structures on private land because this would be illegal. However, Undugu would be willing to provide support and institute an integrated development project like the KPP if the city council or government would allocate them land for resettlement. The villagers were thus left to approach the city and local administrative authorities for alternative sites to rebuild improved slum settlements. Various attempts have been made by the village committee to meet with local administration officials and local politicians, but so far, nothing has been forthcoming.[7]

With its established image as an NGO interested in slum improvement, and with immense access to city and central government authorities (see Appendix A), Undugu is in a good position to intercede for these communities. However, precisely because of its established image as an apolitical organization, it distances itself from these direct negotiations with authorities, notwithstanding its access and potential influence. Some in Undugu view this noncommittal stance as a severe limitation to achieving the organization's goals. Indeed, among the more caustic remarks of one NGO official was that the KPP had outlived its usefulness and may actually perpetuate dependency. It has settled into routine service provision such as school sponsorships for slum children, community health care, and so forth. This is also the image that Undugu has among other NGOs.[8]

Although service provision suggests the end of the road for empowerment goals, a recent episode involving a group of women kiosk operators who had benefited from Undugu's shelter improvement project, entrepreneur skills training, and business loans is illustrative of the potential empowerment effects of purely service and other facilitative programs. This incident also shows how closely Undugu works with state officials during the implementation of its projects. More importantly, it is suggestive of how much Undugu as an organization is removed from direct political opposition to the state, even in arenas where it would legitimately be expected to support its clients when they are threatened by arbitrary state actions. The Gikomba Women Group story, cited here in its entirety as recorded by Undugu in its 1990–91 biennial report, is compelling:

In 1988, one group of twenty (20) women, all living in igloos, approached Undugu for assistance in building better low-cost houses. They participated in leadership training and successfully built dwellings sufficient for them all.

From this achievement, they requested support to set up individual businesses in petty trades like selling vegetables and maize. Small loans were eventually allocated to each, sufficient to buy initial stock and build simple wood-framed structures to protect the goods from rain and sun. The area District Officer (DO) allocated trading places to them at Muoroto near Gikomba market. The women's businesses went well enough for them to repay their loans on the agreed schedule.

In May 1990, Nairobi City Commission *askaris* rather forcefully cleared the shanty village and trading area. The reason given was that the structures put up were illegal, the kiosks in them were unlicensed and that the area was breeding ground for pickpockets who prowled an adjacent bus station. The eviction was sudden, violent and bloody, provoking a mass response from an irate mob which was subdued by police reinforcements using tear gas. The confrontation spilled into the neighbouring Gikomba market and led to the destruction of the kiosks that were operated by the women's group. The women did manage to recover most of their goods.

Without consulting Undugu, the women went to the chief as a group to ask for an alternative site. They were told to wait, but instead, they proceeded to the District Officer with the same request, arguing that their children were in school and they needed regular income. They were again asked to wait. Accompanied by their children, the women went to the Provincial Commissioner's office in the city center with the same request, only to be told by his assistant that they could not expect anything from him as he was not a politician. The women left, stating that they were marching to the President's official residence, State House, to ask him to intervene.

Information about the women's march to State House reached the Provincial Commissioner (PC) who had earlier declined to see them. The women were then intercepted en route and given audience with the PC who permitted them to resume their business operations at Gikomba market on condition that they would not build any permanent structures. This condition, they refused to accept, arguing that the items they sold went bad quickly and needed to be sheltered. As soon as the group went back to their selling sites they contacted Undugu to tell them what they had done and to ask if they could re-negotiate their loans.

Undugu was obviously happy to comply, in view of the situation. The women did confirm that the self-confidence to do what they did on their own resulted from their previous interaction with Undugu. (USK 1992, 17)

Undugu and the Civil Society Thesis

The experience of Undugu elaborated here is somewhat disillusioning for advocates of the thesis that organizations in civil society will oppose repressive states. Despite its immense resources, organizational and mobilizational capacities, and ample opportunities to oppose the Kenyan state, Undugu has been unable or unwilling to do so. This is true even though some of its clients participated in the general societal mobilization against the former single-party state in Kenya and its director led the NGO Network's opposition against the NGO legislation. Undugu's actions are what one would expect of an organization that has chosen to exit or disengage from direct relations with the state. But as is evident throughout this case study, Undugu continues to have close working relations with the Kenyan government in its development programs but promptly disengages when faced with a confrontation.

Undugu has ignored institutional opportunities for political action in opposition to the state, but it has facilitated grassroots action, although it has remained detached from this too. For instance, although Undugu distances itself from actual political maneuvers, its community mobilization efforts are important advancements in empowering grassroots communities. Undugu's training schemes are limited to specific program areas, such as business entrepreneurship or community health, but they cover important areas such as organizational leadership and communication skills. Undugu also does not intervene on behalf of clients when contact with the state is necessary to carry forth local initiatives (for example, licensing requirements for businesses). This enables the community members to apply their skills and develop self-reliance in dealing with state authorities. This mode of operation has enabled community members not only to sustain their business and communal ventures but also to engage in independent action to surmount larger barriers to their initiatives.

Thus, although the political intent of Undugu's work remains unclear, since it remains aloof from the actual political engagements of its client communities, the political effect of its work at the grassroots is evident in the incidents cited above, either in challenging communities to pursue these political avenues to receive aid or in enabling them to do so for the benefit of programs already implemented. The organization itself seeks to remain outside the direct relations between the community and its political authorities, however. Undugu's own description of its position in this equation is instructive:

> The organization has acted as a temporary intermediary between the people and the administration. It has played the role of a facilitator, an organiser, a mobiliser and an advisor . . . to make the community gain the confidence that they are the prime movers of their own destiny; that they are the major actors in dealing with the factors that confront them. (USK 1992, 8)

The experience of the Undugu Society of Kenya therefore repudiates the thesis that civil society organizations directly engage the state on behalf of society to force political reform. Instead, Undugu's concern is with grassroots empowerment. The cumulative effect of income-generating projects that foster independence, of shelter and community improvements that enhance self-esteem, and of leadership skill training that instills self-confidence and civic ability *is* grassroots empowerment. Undugu's experience is therefore an example of the less explicit political engagements of civil society actors. The case of Undugu reveals an organization that does not confront the state, but whose community development work enables its grassroots clients to do so.

As I argued in the introduction, the predominant image of civil society in Africa is that of *organizations* in society. Present understandings of civil society in Africa point to the direct actions of civil society *organizations* as providing the crucial pressure for democratizing reluctant states (Bratton 1989a; Diamond, Linz, and Lipset 1988; Chazan 1992). The Undugu case confounds this understanding. Although Undugu distances itself from explicit political work, it is not unconscious of the underlying political dynamics that keep slum dwellers poor and its role in seeking to alleviate these conditions through grassroots action. Undugu's own critique of the poverty and powerlessness situation in Nairobi's slums and Mbogori's leadership role in the NGO sector (see Chapter 3) indicate that the NGO does not lack an understanding of its role in empowering grassroots communities and as part of the larger NGO community. Undugu was therefore conscious of the democratization agenda and had the resources, organizational ability, and political opportunity to provide a forceful and articulate opposition against the single-party state. Yet Undugu did not emerge as one of the organizations in civil society whose direct oppositional actions forced the undemocratic Moi regime to reform.

The explanation for this can be found in the nature of Undugu as an institutionalized NGO, and especially in its historically fruitful cooperation with the government. As a bureaucratized organization in which overall organizational directions are not personalized (unlike, for example, in the Green Belt Movement) but are instead

sanctioned by governing boards (which include ranking government officials), the degree to which Undugu can mount explicitly
political maneuvers against the state in the name of democratization
is severely limited. The history of fruitful policy cooperation that
Undugu has had with the government (its integration into the system)
blunts its radicalism and limits the speed with which it can respond
to political opportunities such as those that arose between 1990 and
1992 in Kenya. This may explain why Undugu, as an organization in
civil society, remains in a state of stasis even though it is well placed
to influence political movements at both the grassroots and the
national levels.

The main lesson from this case study is that although civil society
organizations may be conscious of their political roles in the democratization movement and may have the resources, capacity, and political opportunity to mobilize, they may still be captives of their own
institutionalization and especially of their connections to the state
they are expected to challenge. Therefore, organizations in civil society that are manifestly beholden to the state (such as favored ethnic
or associational groups) may not be the only ones that are indifferent
or hostile to civil society efforts to directly challenge the undemocratic state. Even seemingly progressive and resourceful organizations
such as Undugu may be unwilling or unable to directly engage the
undemocratic state. Although this case suggests that not all of civil
society participates in organizational challenges against the undemocratic state, it also illustrates the opportunity available to NGOs for
grassroots empowerment.

Notes

1. The following historical discussion is based on information gleaned from
   extensive archival research at the Undugu Society information office.
   Most of the documents consulted were untitled reports with no known
   author. Moreover, since the information was often repeated in many documents, I cited only those documents from which specific information was
   drawn and that are easily accessible. Otherwise, the generic information is
   drawn from various sources that can be found in box files in Undugu's
   information office.
2. Available figures for 1981–84 show a similar expansion in Undugu's
   income: 1981, K Sh 1.9 million (US$67,000); 1982, K Sh 4.6 million
   (US$150,000); 1983, K Sh 9.5 million (US$320,000); 1984, K Sh 6.3 million (US$210,000). For the purposes of illustration and approximation, the
   exchange rate used for this conversion is US$1 = K Sh 30. This may not be
   the exact exchange rate in all years.

3. This is also the period that Undugu underwent organizational restructuring and embarked on its three integrated community development programs. This shift occurred during the tenure of Fabio Dallape (the social scientist) as the executive director.

4. For instance, the Catholic Church's DELTA (Development Educators and Leadership Teams in Action) program was dismantled by the Kenyan government when it was found to have at its core empowerment values driven by the psychosocial educational methods of Paulo Freire and influenced by Latin American-bred liberation theology (personal discussions with Alan Fowler, Kuria Gathuru, and Kabiru Kinyanjui, 1992–93).

5. Some of the material in this section is based on interviews conducted with the following persons in 1992 and 1993: Ezra Mbogori, Director of the Undugu Society of Kenya (1987–92); Kanuku villagers Irungu Ndonga, Monica Kamiti, Gladys Wairimu, and Rosemary Wambua; Kitui villager Mama Ngusie; Kinyago villager Mary Louis Wairimu; Kanuku village headman Runami Thumbi; Kinyago village headman Francis Matoka; Munyisia, Elizabeth, and Kaluki, officials of the Kilumi Women's Group; and Mama Njambi, chair of the Kilumi Women's Group. In addition, I had various interactions with Undugu staff members and Kitui-Pumwani field officers Stella Oduori (social worker), Lucy Nganga (social worker), Nancy Wamea (program coordinator), Musamaria (youth coordinator), and Kuria Gathuru (urban agriculture coordinator). At the Mathare field office, I spoke with Mary Njuguna, Jones, and Kimwadu; and at headquarters with Joyce Ikiara, Lynette Ochola, Martha Muchiri, David Blumenkrantz, and Wanjiku Ndungu of the information office.

6. In this instance, the exchange rate was K Sh 20 = US$1.

7. This was true even in 1992, which was an election year (the first multi-party elections). The slum area, as is much of Nairobi, is solidly behind the opposition parties, and in particular FORD-Asili. The area member of parliament is from FORD-Asili.

8. As determined by private conversations with other NGO actors and lay observers.

Land Improvement over 50 yr lease.
Tree and agric. planting
50 yr tenure / lease. —

5

The Green Belt Movement

THE GREEN BELT MOVEMENT (GBM) is a national grass-roots-based environmental NGO that focuses on mobilizing rural women in tree planting. The GBM takes tree planting as the focal point of advancing the fight against environmental degradation as well as inculcating a broader development ideology and political action that are elaborated by its vocal founder and leader, Wangari Maathai. Indeed, it is difficult to separate the GBM from Maathai. And despite some measure of institutionalization in the NGO (most evident in the routine steps of its tree planting campaign), it is difficult to envisage GBM's work—especially its political work—without the dynamic leadership provided by Maathai.

The GBM has challenged the Kenyan government on specific issues related to the environment as well as on general issues related to governance, such as human rights and political prisoners. The GBM's involvement in the agitation for political reform in Kenya epitomizes the civil society thesis—that organizations in civil society are important actors in forcing the African state to reform its governance structures. However, although the GBM underscores this celebrated vision of civil society's opposition to the state, the centrality of the person of Wangari Maathai in its actions reveals a twofold reality that may ultimately undermine civil society's promise of altering the fundamental power relations between African states and their citizens. The first reality is that political actions by individual civil society organizations are ignited by the organization's leadership; second is that this leadership is *personal* and, though largely benevolent, is ultimately unaccountable.

The GBM today consists of over 50,000 members organized in over 2,000 local community groups in twenty-seven of the forty-two administrative districts in Kenya. These groups are focused on tree planting: they maintain over 1,000 active tree nurseries in which they raise seedlings and issue them free of charge to local farmers and public institutions such as schools, hospitals, and churches. In turn, the GBM supports the running of the nurseries by providing basic farm implements and, most importantly, by paying the women's groups for every surviving tree that they raise and issue to area farmers and institutions. Through its grassroots network of affiliated women's groups and their tree nurseries, the GBM has planted over 10 million trees in Kenya since its inception in 1977. These trees have been planted mainly by individual farmers on their small farms and by others in public woodlots, such as at schools or hospitals in rural areas. In so doing, the GBM has pushed back the spread of environmental degradation in the rural areas, which stems mainly from deforestation. The GBM has also enabled communities to reap the benefits of balanced tree harvesting and provided additional income and employment opportunities to rural women involved in its tree-planting campaign. On the "production" front, then, the GBM has much to commend it as an environmental NGO, despite accusations from critics that all it plants are billboards.[1]

Less tangible, but equally evident throughout my field studies, is the degree of grassroots mobilization and political consciousness that the GBM has fostered in participating communities. The deceptively simple activity of tree planting undertaken by semiliterate rural women has provided an appropriate entry point not just for environmental education but also for consciousness-raising about national political realities and for empowerment. Because it relies on local expertise—"rural women as foresters"—and responds to local needs (such as lack of fuel wood), and also because it generates income for the members, the GBM's tree planting campaign is an important tool in the social and economic empowerment of these communities. By demonstrating the self-reliance and capacity of rural women and by increasing their capacity through income generation (and thus restoring some measure of control over their lives), the GBM enhances the women's felt power. Alongside the mundane activities of tree planting, the GBM has held hundreds of community seminars to educate members on environmental initiatives and to broaden their minds on national social, economic, and political realities.

Sensitizing rural women to the local environment and enabling them to raise seedlings, involving them in promoting tree planting and, through these activities, educating them on the immediate local and national social, economic, and political realities have enhanced member groups' awareness about broader political issues. More importantly, the GBM's actions at the national level and, in particular, its outright challenges to the state on various projects it regards as being environmentally shortsighted or against the public interest have furthered the political consciousness of its membership. From my interactions with the grassroots membership, it was evident that although GBM members are not directly involved in its "larger than rural life" engagements with the state (for example, the Uhuru Park confrontation), they are acutely aware of the issues involved and are strongly committed to what Maathai does at the national level. This identification and solidarity with GBM's politicized engagements are most evident in the exuberant support that one can witness at the GBM's annual general meetings, which bring together over 400 representatives countrywide. More importantly, the members' support is evident in the continued "production" activities at the grassroots, despite official harassment and intimidation.

The GBM's contribution to evolving state–society relations and, in particular, its close association with the progressive democratic forces in Kenya stem from the fact that it has exploited the grassroots organization and socioeconomic empowerment it fosters through its production activities. The extensive network of independent grassroots women's groups that form the GBM provides an important channel for political education, and the GBM leadership has used this channel directly or indirectly to raise the political awareness of its members and their local communities. The GBM has treated this network and the benign activity of planting trees as a vehicle for education, particularly on local and national social and political issues (Maathai 1992).

One example that I discuss at some length in this chapter is how the GBM utilized its tree planting grassroots networks to further a general, decidedly political mobilization for a civic education campaign prior to Kenya's first postindependence multiparty general elections in 1992. This suggests the GBM's ability and *willingness* to seize available opportunities to undermine the undemocratic state— or, more specifically, the Moi regime. This civic education initiative also sets the GBM apart from many indigenous NGOs in Kenya (such as Undugu) that have comparable mobilization capacities and resources but did not take advantage of the political opportunity.

This is further evidence of the GBM's prominent place in civil society in Kenya, in shaping state–civil society relations, and in contributing to the advancement of the democratization process. The GBM experience seems to fit the predominant expectations of the role of civil society institutions in democratization. The GBM has a conscious grassroots empowerment agenda (Fowler 1991b) and has exploited its *institutional* resources and mobilization capacity (Bratton 1989a) and the available political opportunity (Tarrow 1991). However, the confirmatory power of the GBM case, when viewed against the confounding case of Undugu, begs further explanation. For the moment, the institutional stasis argument I advanced for Undugu's case will suffice. But as will become evident in this chapter, the important variables explaining civil society's support of democratization are not limited to what the previous cases (Chapters 3 and 4) confirm (that is, political opportunity, organization and resources, and alliances); they include a more arbitrary element of personal leadership. This, as I argue in the concluding chapter, raises questions about where the political power of NGOs derives from and, even more importantly, where it resides. The answers have important implications for the extent to which NGOs and other resourceful actors in civil society can be expected to alter the fundamental organization of power in African societies.

History and Growth of the Movement[2]

The Green Belt Movement was started in 1977 by the National Council of Women of Kenya (NCWK)[3] as the "Save the Land Harambee," in response to the threat of desertification in Kenya. Participants were expected to pull together to check the threat of desertification by planting trees. The project was led by an enthusiastic Wangari Maathai, who had already distinguished herself as the first woman Ph.D. and university professor in Kenya. Maathai had also just been nominated and elected to the NCWK national executive to head its environment committee (Maathai [1980]).

The Save the Land Harambee tree planting campaign was launched in a ceremony marking World Environment Day in June 1977. Seven trees were planted at the Kamukunji Grounds in Nairobi in honor of seven legendary men and women who had made significant contributions to Kenya's history. Of these seven trees, only two survived; nevertheless, the initiative spawned a permanent tree planting campaign. The NCWK propagated tree planting through its network of affiliate organizations, and, at the invitation of local communities, representatives traveled to rural districts to spread the environmental message and plant trees with community members. In the same year, the United Nations held its Conference on Desertification in Nairobi, and this added impetus to the infant tree planting campaign. At the NCWK's instigation, conference delegates planted a "green belt" on a women's cooperative farm in Naivasha. This was among the very first green belts—a woodlot of at least 1,000 trees. The name Green Belt was later adopted by the fledgling NGO as an apt image of its work in reforesting the land (Maathai [1980], 1988).

At this initial stage, the NCWK's tree planting campaign received seedlings free of charge from the national network of tree nurseries run by the Forestry Department under the Ministry of Environment and Natural Resources. As the campaign gathered momentum, its demands for seedlings outstripped the government's ability to provide them free, and a small fee was charged (Maathai [1980], 1988). In the early 1980s, the GBM emerged as an independent organization but retained close links with the NCWK. Most importantly, it retained almost all the NCWK members on its executive board. To enhance its independence, the GBM sought ways to raise its own seedlings as part of a year-round campaign of planting trees. Furthermore, under the full-time direction of its founder-coordinator, the GBM was slowly evolving a broader development ethic that sought to impact the lives of rural women in more fundamental ways than just galvanizing periodic tree planting efforts.

Today, under the continued leadership of Maathai, the GBM has established itself as one of the largest (in terms of grassroots spread) and most prominent indigenous NGOs in Kenya. It has an extensive network of local affiliated groups running their own tree nurseries and issuing seedlings to individual farmers and institutions. Apart from its record 10 million-plus trees planted, evidence of the GBM's success includes the numerous international awards that the movement and Maathai have received for environmental work and political activism. At the grassroots, it has steadily educated and raised the consciousness of its members about the sociopolitical issues of the day. At the national level, it has been an unrelenting defender of the environment and the public interest, especially against the single-party KANU regime in the late 1980s. The success of the GBM's tree planting campaign in Kenya and its activism has inspired efforts to expand it through the formation of Green Belt International and a Pan-African Green Belt Movement (PAGBM), which has resulted in attempts to replicate the GBM's work in a number of African countries.[4]

The cornerstone of the GBM's short- and long-term objectives is empowering local communities to respond to local needs. To this end, the GBM attempts to place local communities at the center of defining their problems, searching for solutions, and acting to counteract them (Maathai 1988, 9). The GBM espouses over twenty specific objectives, most of which revolve around ways of improving and conserving the environment, especially trees. Interwoven within these objectives of restoring the environment is an important empowerment agenda: "to encourage participants to empower themselves, strengthen their self-confidence and self-esteem" by promoting a positive image of women in national development; by giving them training, information, and a voice to articulate needs and preferences through various forums; and by supplementing incomes (Maathai 1988, 9; see also Maathai [1980]; GBM n.d.a). These empowerment goals are similar to the ones articulated by Undugu, especially the focus on the individual as the point of intervention and anticipated action.

How the Green Belt Movement Works

The basic idea behind the GBM's grassroots-driven tree planting campaign is that women's groups in rural areas raise tree seedlings and give them to farmers and institutions free of charge. The women's groups are then paid a small amount per surviving tree by the GBM secretariat. As a grassroots-based NGO, the GBM is driven by the active participation of its members at the local level in all its activities. The local groups are linked to a national secretariat in Nairobi, where group activities are monitored by a coordinator (Maathai) and a staff of about twenty "monitors." In addition, there are about 800 field-workers—nursery attendants, area advisors, and district representatives—who monitor field activities. An executive board of six to eight volunteers meets periodically to set and oversee the GBM's overall goals and programs; about half of the board is made up of representatives of the NCWK, many of whom have been on the board since the GBM's founding.

The GBM's lack of institutionalization is underscored by a conspicuous absence of icons such as a permanent headquarters or bureaucratic procedures (except for payment procedures). Since being evicted by the government from prefabricated offices at the city center (opposite the University of Nairobi main campus) following the Uhuru Park confrontation in 1989, the GBM has operated out of Maathai's three-bedroom bungalow in a middle-class estate. The files and monitors are housed in a wooden shed built on the compound and in Maathai's converted garage and veranda. The living room—an unassuming clutter of rugs, books, memorabilia, and awards—is where Maathai meets with the executive board, grassroots members from rural areas, international dignitaries, politicians, and other notables. She is hounded occasionally by the police and has been arrested for "subversive activities."

Indeed, the only tangible icon of institutionalization in the GBM is the routine of tree planting. The GBM runs on a fairly simple step-by-step process from the initial formation of a member group to the issuing of tree seedlings. The first step entails group formation. In this respect, the GBM does not go out to form groups or establish tree nurseries in rural communities; instead, it awaits a formal invitation from interested parties. The GBM may undertake initial publicity campaigns organized by the national secretariat or by existing GBM groups in the area, but the initiative must come from the community itself so that the nurseries can be self-sustaining. Once a request for membership is received (and normally all requests are accepted), the GBM secretariat offers orientation seminars to the interested group. This orientation includes a comprehensive ten-step procedure that forms the GBM's modus operandi, which is summarized here.[5]

Following the orientation, the second step is to undertake a public awareness campaign to educate the local community about local environmental degradation, sustainable development alternatives, and the benefits of planting trees. One focus of this public awareness campaign is on localized deprivations stemming from unsound uses of the local environment or "development with destruction" (Maathai 1993). Such an environmental message couched in local terms and anchored in local situations is more likely to receive sympathetic attention than technical environmental information. This awareness campaign also enables the group to assess the need for trees in the area so that it will be able to supply the seedlings and ensure success for the planned project.

After the public education campaign, the group is ready to start its own tree nursery. This involves a tedious routine of collecting seeds, making seedbeds, planting, daily watering, and transplanting young seedlings to individual plastic bags. A particularly important aspect of this routine is keeping detailed and accurate records on the number and types of seedlings (indigenous, exotic, fruits). Each tree nursery employs a young person (preferably a young woman) as a nursery attendant who performs the daily chores. The GBM secretariat pays the nursery attendant a small stipend and provides some basic tools for the upkeep of the nursery, such as water tanks, hoes, rakes, and plastic bags for retaining seedlings. Usually the women's group meets at least once a week to work on the nursery and update records. For example, they weed the seedbeds, arrange and recount seedlings, collect new seeds, or issue seedlings when they are ready. The group also deliberates on its progress and sends progress reports to the secretariat.

Around the time that seedlings are ready to be transplanted into farms, the women's group intensifies its promotion of tree planting in the surrounding community. Besides speaking to farmers and public institutions (for example, schools and hospitals), the groups are supposed to ensure that those who have agreed to plant the seedlings make adequate preparations (such as digging appropriate holes) to ensure the survival of the trees. After this promotion campaign and after ensuring that the farmers are ready to receive the trees, the group issues its seedlings to the recipients free of charge. This is an important milestone for every tree nursery but is by no means the final stage in the campaign. Immediately after issuing the seedlings, the women have to follow up on the trees to ascertain that the recipients planted them and took appropriate steps to ensure their survival (for example, watered, manured, and protected young trees from browsing animals). This initial follow-up is repeated a number of times until a final follow-up is made two to three months after the trees were issued. At this stage, all surviving trees are counted, and the information is forwarded to the secretariat for the group's payment to be processed.

In all these steps, it is the group members—most of them illiterate or semiliterate women—who are involved in carrying out the activities. Indeed, at every step of the way, the women's groups have to compile data on their major activities (collecting seeds, planting, issuing seedlings) and forward this information to the secretariat on the designated forms. Only after the secretariat has perused the forwarded documents for consistency and accuracy can the group expect to receive any payment. And only after the final follow-up of surviving trees is made and reported to the secretariat will full payment be made to the group. This whole process—from initiating a tree nursery to issuing trees and receiving final payment for the same—should ideally be completed in six months.

Money for supporting the women's groups in this way is the GBM's greatest need. So far, however, the NGO has been unable to generate its own income. The GBM does not sell its seedlings to the public, since this would undermine the goal of encouraging people to plant more trees—charging peasant farmers for trees would hinder the reforestation program. Conversely, asking rural African women to volunteer to reforest the land would only add to their already heavy burdens. The GBM has therefore been forced to rely almost exclusively on foreign donor funding and has no illusions of becoming financially self-sustaining in the near future (Maathai 1988, 37–38). Efforts to raise funds locally have been unfruitful, largely because of the GBM's high-profile political activism.

At its inception in 1977 as an NCWK project, the GBM relied on the umbrella organization for funding and received some limited support from the private sector, such as Mobil Oil (Kenya) (Maathai 1988; Mbaya 1993). As it evolved into a permanent and sustainable movement in the 1980s, the GBM was able to attract more consistent funding from abroad, which enabled it to expand its tree planting activities to more districts. Compared with the Undugu Society of Kenya, however, the GBM's financial outlays are very small. The projected 1993 budget stood at K Sh 5 million (US$77,000) (Mbaya 1993). A nearly three-year projection for 1988–90 totaled only K Sh 6.6 million (US$101,000), with average annual expenditures of K Sh 2.2 million (US$34,000).[6] Similarly, for 1991, the total budgetary projections were K Sh 3.3 million (US$51,000). Fifty percent of the total income is devoted to tree planting activities (group payments and inputs), 22 percent to educational and training seminars, and 28 percent to administration.[7]

The GBM has had only a few major donors, with a number of them giving large one-time grants for activities in a number of districts—as is the practice with project aid (see Appendix B). The most consistent donors have offered renewable grants that support a substantial part of the GBM's tree planting campaign countrywide. The Royal Norwegian Embassy Development Cooperation (NORAD) was one of the GBM's largest donors until 1990, when Kenya broke off diplomatic relations with Norway (*Weekly Review,* October 26, 1990).[8] Since then, the Netherlands Organization for International Development Cooperation (NOVIB) has been the largest recurrent donor to the GBM. Indeed, NOVIB seems to have fashioned a truly compatible partnership with the GBM among a number of its local NGO partners. NOVIB is intensely involved in environmental issues as well as in the areas of women's rights and human rights and does a lot of lobbying both at home and in the international arena.

The emerging relationship between NOVIB and the GBM may be important in further institutionalizing the GBM as an important actor in civil society in Kenya, especially in the furtherance of the democratization process. In the 1980s, NOVIB supported a number of NGOs pursuing disparate activities, including the Breastfeeding Information Group (BIG), Kenya Consumer Organization (KCO), Africa Refugees Education Program (AREP), Public Law Institute, and GBM. However, in a new program of action for 1993–96, NOVIB emphasizes three themes: the environment, human rights, and women. More specifically, it has spelled out a commitment to only those local NGOs that will focus on issues and advocacy relating to human rights, democracy, and economic policy review (*Novib News,* January 1993).

GBM Achievements

From the paltry seven trees planted in 1977—only two of which survived—the GBM has sustained the tree planting campaign and planted over 10 million trees, with a survival rate of 75 percent.[9] In 1986, the

GBM was estimated to have reached over 6,700 rural homesteads (an estimated 40,000 people) through over 600 tree nurseries that had distributed a total of 750,000 trees to private holdings and 330,000 trees to over 500 public institutions. A total of 1,080,000 trees had been planted, with 850,000 of these surviving. Available figures indicate that an even greater number of tress have been planted in subsequent years. For example, in the six-month period between September 1990 and April 1991, under a NORAD grant, the GBM planted 1.9 million trees, of which 1.3 million survived. Under another grant in 1991–92, 1.8 million trees were planted, of which 1.6 million survived.[10]

The GBM has thus continued to expand in terms of the number of trees issued and planted through its efforts. In some areas, especially the central province districts, the GBM has become well established; in newer areas of operation, the growth of the GBM has been tremendous. For instance, in Nyandarua district, a newly settled area of cleared forests, the number of GBM tree nurseries grew from four in 1987 to seventy-five in 1992. In those five years, these nurseries issued about 1.4 million trees, with over half of them issued between 1991 and 1992 (see Table 5.1).

Apart from helping to expand the tree cover in rural districts, the GBM has also supplemented the incomes of its members and provided employment to over 800 rural people, mostly as nursery attendants, advisors, and promoters of tree planting in their local communities. Even more important, it has provided additional income to individual members of women's groups through payments for surviving trees issued to local farmers and institutions. Groups are paid two Kenyan shillings (approximately US$0.03) for every surviving tree. Although the amount per seedling is small, it adds up when one considers how many surviving trees an active tree nursery could have to its credit every year.

According to my own calculations, based on the actual 1992 figures from active tree nurseries in Nyandarua district (see Table 5.1), an individual member could expect to receive over K Sh 800 (approximately US$12) a year:

Number of surviving trees paid for	243,921
Number of tree nurseries (TN)	75
Average number of surviving trees per TN	3,252[11]
Average expected payment per TN	K Sh 6,504 (US$97)
Estimated average number of TN members	8
Estimated average income per member	K Sh 813 (US$12)

Given that the average annual income for a rural household is less than US$400, this additional income is an important incentive for

Table 5.1 Productivity in GBM Nurseries in Nyandarua District, 1987–92

	1987	1988	1989	1990	1991	1992
Number of tree nurseries	4	9	11	15	49	75
Number of field staff (nursery attendants and advisors)	3	9	10	11	32	43
Number of trees issued	5,362	108,479	174,877	264,789	315,159	524,264
Number of surviving trees paid for (excludes disputed trees)*	8,000	8,000	18,098	44,724	218,546	243,921

* The number of trees paid for may exceed the number issued because of payments made for trees issued in the preceding year.

Source: "General Report Nyandarua District 1987–1992," prepared by Njogu Kahare, Nyandarua district advisor, 1992.

GBM members to continue participating in the movement, especially since there is little input cost apart from their labor and active participation. This incentive has contributed to the success of the GBM's tree planting campaign, and especially to the high rate of tree survival that has been achieved. The fact that the final payment for trees is dependent on the number surviving places the responsibility of ensuring tree survival on the group, more so than if it was simply off-loading seedlings. Similarly, the recipient farmer also bears more responsibility than if he or she had just bought the seedlings at a subsidized price or received them freely without any follow-up supervision, which is the case with government-sponsored programs. It is important to remember that the women's group–farmer transaction occurs within a fairly small rural community where the group and its tree nursery are one of the local social institutions, such as a school committee, women's guild, or other *harambee* initiative. Within this context, the recipient farmer is likely to uphold his or her social obligation to ensure the trees' survival so that the group will be paid. Giving both the recipient and the giver a stake in the outcome is an innovative way of ensuring the trees' survival.

The GBM's tree-planting campaign has been a success on several counts. In particular, it is a sustainable program of tree planting, since community tree nurseries are not one-time affairs but continuous in production. The semivoluntary nature of the GBM's campaign makes it affordable for rural women to participate without overburdening them further. The immediate benefits of tree harvesting (fuelwood, fencing material, fodder) are themselves incentives for participating in and continuing the tree planting campaign. Women are not just planters of trees but also promoters of their own communities. The GBM's tree-planting campaign is also replicable, as evidenced by its expansion across Kenya and more recently to other African countries.[12]

The GBM's success can be measured not only by the number of tree nurseries produced or the number of trees planted, but also by the impact it has had on its members and, more broadly, on state-society relations in Kenya. In this regard, the GBM's tree planting campaign has enhanced the leadership skills of its grassroots membership not only through its regular training sessions but also through the active grassroots participation in all stages of the campaign. These activities require skills in group organization and decision making as well as skill and courage to counter intimidation that may be experienced in the field from local government officials (for example, chiefs)—especially when the GBM national leadership is involved in periodic wrangles with the state.

The GBM and the National Council of Churches of Kenya have been the most vocal NGOs in Kenya. This was especially so in the late 1980s, when the single-party state had rendered many of the indigenous organizations in civil society ineffective and suppressed other independent or dissenting voices. What predisposed the GBM to political engagements with the state, especially at a time when many other actors in the NGO community and in civil society remained mute? To explain this propensity to protest and advocacy, one needs to examine the GBM's working philosophy. Its protest and advocacy work in the late 1980s is actually the result of an unfolding working philosophy and the progression of its programmatic goals on the ground—from production activities to empowerment. Thus the GBM's protest and advocacy actions at the institutional level are an integral part of the evolution of the mundane activities of tree planting at the grassroots. The organization's activities in civil society are also made possible by this base of mobilized networks at the grassroots.

The GBM's Working Philosophy

The GBM views Africa's environmental degradation as resulting from the imperatives of "modern development," which remain blind to the long-term environmental implications of "development with destruction" (Maathai 1993). What the GBM espouses, along with many other development practitioners, is "sustainable development," which safeguards the environment for the future. Below is an exemplary critique that emerged from discussions in a GBM seminar as an illustrative case of development with destruction:

> A community of coffee farmers drains a natural swamp to use the waterlogged soil for making bricks to build "modern" brick houses. These modern houses cannot be complete without roofs of corrugated iron sheets, which have to be bought from industries in the urban areas, where the raw materials are most likely imported. By this simple act of acquiring an icon of modernity as prescribed by the prevailing social belief of what development entails, this rural community has established a local dependency on the urban area and helped perpetuate the national economy's dependency on international markets. More importantly, it has most likely instigated a vicious circle of environmental degradation and poverty. Thus, the corrugated iron factory (which most likely pollutes the environment) also demands foreign exchange for raw material imports; therefore, the coffee farmer has to produce more coffee (a monocultural practice that exhausts the soil and reduces the acreage used to produce food) for export to earn more foreign exchange for the country; at the same time, the drying up of the swamp may affect the local ecosystem and, in particular, lead to reduced rainfall, resulting in a decline in food and coffee production and in the productivity of the land, the human population, and the local and national economies. Without sufficient food production, the community sinks into greater depths of impoverishment but with beautiful brick houses to show for its modernity.[13]

This critique is especially pertinent for the GBM as an NGO focusing on women, since women are the prominent managers and workers of the land in Kenya and in much of Africa. For example, women fetch water and fuelwood for their households, work the land, and market the produce, as well as tend to their typically large families. Women are also the first to suffer the various manifestations of environmental degradation and the resultant impoverishment (Maathai 1993). To them, environmental degradation has an immediate effect on their daily lives: they have to fetch water and fuelwood from afar, bring in meager harvests from their land, and invest more time and energy to supplement their families' food—including waiting in food lines in times of famine. One cannot focus on the environment in rural communities without paying attention to those who are most immediately touched by its degradation. The environmental movement in Kenya, the GBM believes, cannot ignore the position of women in society. Moreover, beyond this critique of the social position of women in Kenya, the GBM's working philosophy entails a critique of the marginal *political* position of the masses of citizens in Kenya and in the developing world in general (see Maathai 1991). Thus, the environmental movement as espoused by the GBM becomes a political movement.

Maathai affirms this expansive working philosophy of her environmental movement: "Once you start making these linkages, you can no longer do just tree planting. When you start working with the environment seriously, the whole arena comes: human rights, women's rights, environmental rights, children's rights . . . everybody's rights" (French 1992). Indeed, in a separate interview, Maathai reaffirms the ultimate political nature of the environmental movement, especially in the context of the ongoing wave of democratization: "The environmental movement has become part and parcel of the pro-democracy movement" (Hultman 1992b, 3).

The GBM's expansive and critical working philosophy is condensed into the simple, practical, and participatory activity of tree planting. The GBM takes the tree-planting campaign both as an end in itself (environmental reclamation) and as a means to an end (empowerment): "When we plant trees in Kenya we know that we will eventually have our hands on politics, on economics, on culture, on all aspects that either destroy or create a sustainable environment" (Maathai in Hultman 1992a, 2). First and foremost, the GBM seeks to help rural women respond to their most immediate needs such as fuelwood, building and fencing materials, pasture, and water and soil conservation. Planting trees fulfills or supplements these immediate needs in a fairly short time. Linking the broader environmental message to local situations and local needs that the rural women can easily relate to attracts and attaches them to the wider GBM cause. The simple activity of planting trees enables rural communities to understand local environmental degradation and their capacity to contribute to its restoration and preservation.

Inasmuch as the tree planting campaign fulfills some immediate needs (for example, income and fuel resources), it represents an important step toward enhancing the capacity for independent action by rural women. This process is further enhanced by the leadership training that the women's groups are exposed to. The GBM treats the grassroots activities around tree planting as an entry point for a much broader campaign to raise its members' awareness of their social, economic, and political disadvantages and to empower them through information and education. In moving from one level to the next, tree planting remains the focal activity and the local community the focal ground. The environmental message can be linked to local problem situations, such as the clearing of forests for farming and the lack of firewood. It can also be linked to the insensitive public policies (such as the clearing of natural forests or the eviction of forest dwellers) of unresponsive and unaccountable governments. At both levels, the GBM stresses that local community action can stem such problems. Thus, community members can plant trees and also challenge unpopular state actions at the local level.

The GBM's critical view of what the environmental movement entails within the sociopolitical context in Kenya and its pursuant actions have brought it into conflict with the Kenyan government on a number of occasions. Because of these conflicts, the GBM has emerged as the most unpopular NGO with the Moi government. This was not always the case, however. Indeed, GBM-government relations were amicable in its early years. When the GBM operated as the Save the Land Harambee under the NCWK, it received all its seedlings from the government's Forestry Department free of charge (Maathai [1980]). Moreover, the GBM sought to foster these cordial relations by requiring all groups that wanted to join the movement to have at least three local leaders (for example, the area member of parliament, an administrative officer such as the local district officer, and the chief) on the groups' governing committees. Similarly, at many public events, such as the launching of new tree nurseries or the planting of new public green belts, high-ranking government officials and politicians were invited as guests of honor (see "Save Our Trees" [1982], 7; Maathai [1980]). As late as 1986, the GBM was the only NGO appointed to serve on the National Environmental Committee alongside the minister, assistant minister, and permanent secretary in the Ministry of Environment and Natural Resources and senior government officials from the National Environmental Secretariat. This body was supposed to come up with a national environmental policy and intervention program for the government.

However, in the mid-1980s, the GBM started to experience problems with the government, especially as Maathai became more outspoken. Indeed, there is no evidence to suggest that GBM representatives attended subsequent meetings of the National Environmental Committee, although relations with the National Environmental Secretariat continued, albeit at a decidedly lower ebb. Other factors suggest that by the mid-1980s the GBM was drawing further and further away from the government. Between 1984 and 1985, the GBM made spirited efforts to acquire one of many government-owned vacant lots in Nairobi on which to build a headquarters. These efforts included writing letters to the minister of environment and natural resources and, ultimately, to President Moi. However, all this was to no avail—perhaps one of the first indications that the government was becoming wary of the GBM's independence and activity. It is instructive to note that NGOs and other organizations that were identified as pro-government had received resources or favorable treatment from the government. For instance, in 1988, the president canceled a K Sh 6 million (US$90,000) income tax debt owed by *Maendeleo ya Wanawake* (the national women's organization then affiliated with KANU) with respect to its city center building. This was no doubt due to its pro-government stance, which was most evident in its later condemnation of Maathai as an errant woman who was disrespectful of national elders when she opposed government plans to build a skyscraper at Uhuru Park.

It is evident that the GBM was supported by the government in its initial years because it appeared to be a benign women's organization volunteering to plant trees. However, when it grew independent and dared to challenge the state on certain issues (unlike other NGOs at the time), it became a threat to the government. Maathai's explanation of the radical shift in GBM-government relations suggests that this shift coincided with the transition that the GBM was making from meeting the local needs of rural women to progressively empowering them:

> In the initial stages, paternalistic governments do not feel threatened by the simple issue of tree planting by rural women—no government wants to be seen as being anti-environment but in the course of its activities and especially [community] education and experiences, GBM "steps on toes." Then they [government] say it is dangerous—sooner or later people will understand the issues and act. (Maathai 1993; see also Topouzis 1990, 31)

The GBM's environmental campaign, begun as a benign movement, soon found itself at loggerheads with the government because most of the problems it addresses originate from policy or political decisions—for example, damming a river, evicting forest dwellers, or clearing forests. For this reason, Maathai has taken an approach that calls for engagement with the government, when necessary, as a starting point toward correcting local environmental degradation.

Opportunities for Protest and Advocacy

In the Kenyan NGO community, the Green Belt Movement under Wangari Maathai stands out as a vehemently political NGO that has spared no opportunity to challenge the state on issues that it considers within its purview or within the broader public interest. Apart from the mundane tasks of its permanent tree planting campaign, the GBM has been a prominent actor pursuing advocacy and protest from the late 1980s to the present. Policy advocacy is not a recent development for the GBM nor is a confrontational stance the only method it has used. Prior to 1986, when GBM-government relations were more amicable, the GBM sought to ally with government efforts at tree planting and to influence policy within the forums accessible to it, such as the National Environment Secretariat and the National Environment Committee. However, due partly to the single-party state's suppression of private voluntary agencies and other independent actors in civil society, the GBM evolved a more confrontational stance after realizing that there was little possibility of achieving policy influence amicably.

The GBM's advocacy pursuits have ranged from simply writing to the local government administration and questioning actions, such as the indiscriminate cutting of trees in local areas, to voicing strong public objections to plans to convert public parks in Nairobi to underground parking, private plots, or office complexes. These actions have included opposing certain environmentally unfriendly development plans, many of which have been propagated by the KANU government (then a single-party entity) or by private developers with the support of or links to the former. Such public protests or advocacy efforts were invariably perceived as outright challenges to the state and to the Moi regime. The Uhuru Park confrontation discussed in Chapter 3 is one example. Two recent incidents further suggest that the GBM has established itself as a champion of what it deems the public interest and, moreover, is seen by many citizens as such.

The first incident concerns the Jeevanjee's Gardens, a public park of about five acres that was a gift to the city of Nairobi from a prominent Asian business family in the colonial era. Situated within the city center, the Jeevanjee's Gardens are a favorite spot for lunchtime relaxation and for street preachers. In early 1991, the local press unveiled plans by the government-appointed city commission (which had replaced the elected city council beginning in 1982) to allocate the gardens to an unnamed private developer for the construction of a shopping mall and an underground parking complex. Much debate ensued on this proposal, with many Nairobi citizens, including the descendants of the Jeevanjee family, vehemently opposing the development plans. Much of this protest was carried out by private citizens writing to the government; others expressed their opinions in the "Letters to the Editor" page of national dailies.

At the instigation of associates of the Jeevanjee family, the GBM added its voice to the opposition, basing its stand on the environmental shortsightedness of the plans. The GBM was a particularly useful ally, and its entry may have tilted the balance in favor of those opposing the development plans. It added prominence to the debate because of its previous engagement with the state on the Uhuru Park complex. (Incidentally, the Uhuru Park project stalled when its financiers withdrew and the government moved to dismantle the fence that had surrounded the proposed site—a quiet vindication of the GBM's success.) A few weeks and more outcries later, the plans to develop the Jeevanjee's Gardens into a commercial complex were shelved following a presidential decree.

A similar fiasco, but of lesser proportions, ensued regarding plans to open up for commercial exploitation a three-mile-long seafront stretch of land overlooking the main channel into the Mombasa harbor. The Mama Ngina Drive (named after Kenya's first first lady) and the surrounding land are dotted with a number of historical sites, making the area a favorite weekend relaxation spot for Mombasa residents. The first indication of possible plans to convert this public land to private use was given by a ministerial order contained in the *Kenya Gazette*[14] declassifying the area as a preserved historical site. There was an immediate outcry from some Mombasa residents, though no plans had been announced to develop the area. Again, much of the public complaint was expressed in the "Letters to the Editor" section of the national dailies. Some residents enlisted the GBM's aid in opposing the plans. As the controversy wore on, the GBM issued a press statement condemning the government's plans, arguing that such plans were against the public interest, which the government was supposed to uphold. Once again, after additional outcries, the government moved to reclassify the Mama Ngina Drive area as a historical site of national importance, therefore foreclosing any planned privatization or private development.

Although the GBM did not initiate or carry the mantle of these protests by itself, its institutional involvement demonstrated its commitment to advocacy and protest on behalf of the defenseless public interest. Moreover, the fact that in both cases and in other similar ones private citizens solicited the GBM's support and voice is an indication of the public's regard for the movement as one of the few institutions in civil society that is able and willing to stand up to the government and oppose actions that are inimical to the public interest.

Admittedly, in all the above initiatives (including the Uhuru Park saga), there was little or no direct involvement of the grassroots membership of the GBM. These campaigns required writing numerous letters to government officials, issuing press statements, instituting civil suits, or lobbying private developers and financiers both local and international. Much of this was pursued by Maathai, especially because her name commands recognition and attention, if not clout. However, many other localized efforts have been in the hands of local members, usually with the backing of the secretariat and especially Maathai. More importantly, the continuous commitment of the grassroots membership to GBM initiatives and their continued production activities, despite the political wrangles between the GBM and the government or the more personal Moi-Maathai chasm, indicate their solidarity with the GBM cause. For instance, very few groups, especially in those areas where the GBM is most established, abandoned their activities despite intimidation by the local manifestation of the overbearing state—the local chief—and the leadership of *Maendeleo ya Wanawake* at the height of GBM-government confrontations.[15]

One of the more recent political actions that the GBM embarked on and one that involved a greater degree of grassroots participation was a civic education campaign conducted prior to the December 1992 multiparty general elections—the first such elections since independence in 1963. The civic education campaign was an important undertaking, since the transition to a multiparty system was in many ways incomplete, especially given that the repressive structures and culture of the single-party state were still intact due to the intransigence of the former sole political party (KANU). After nearly thirty years of single-party authoritarian rule, the transition to political pluralism also presented problems of adjustment for the electorate. The GBM believed that voter apathy and fear of the state, as well as a lack of knowledge about political pluralism, would undermine the possibility of having free and fair polls (Maathai interviews and public presentations 1992).

Although there was much public euphoria over the new political freedom, a widespread suspicion and apathy persisted regarding the potential veracity of forthcoming elections. Previous experiences with single-party elections had demonstrated the state's lack of respect for the power of the vote. For instance, the 1988 general elections were believed to have been rigged. These had been the first national elections to employ a controversial queue voting method that had voters line up behind the candidate of their choice. Massive rigging and voter intimidation marked this poorly attended election, defying the much publicized logic of it being a more open and transparent method than the secret ballot. Although the secret ballot was restored for the 1992 multiparty elections, there was nonetheless a widespread belief that the besieged KANU regime was intent on rigging and had already laid the groundwork for this. Among the actions that critics cited as compromising the forthcoming elections was the KANU government's unilateral appointment of the electoral commission that would supervise the polls, order and store the ballot papers, conduct the voter registration, and count the votes (see various issues of *Society* [August–December 1992]).

The icons of the repressive state remained even as other indications suggested a more open political system. For instance, detention laws, licensing requirements for political rallies, the secret police, and ethnic violence in sections of the country, as well as political prisoners languishing in prisons, all made it difficult to believe that the political changes were complete and irreversible. There was widespread election-related violence and various mushrooming "operation" groups that mobilized different sections of the population to support competing political parties (see *Society*, [August–December 1992]). Those associated with KANU were first thought to be out to instigate violence, but they later emerged as equally disruptive conduits of "pouring money" to canvass for votes countrywide. The prevailing insecurity contributed to the fear of the state and intimidation of voters. This atmosphere was likely to intimidate rural voters who had had little exposure to state-society clashes, such as the street demonstrations and riots in the urban areas that preceded the political changes.

Finally, since neither the government nor its appointed electoral commission made any serious effort to educate voters on the facts and the implications of the transition to multiparty politics or to prepare them for the forthcoming elections, many voters were ignorant of the various registration and voting requirements. Given what was happening in the run-up to the elections (including campaign violence, persistent rumors of rigging, and other electoral malpractices such as vote buying), the GBM believed that the possibility for free and fair democratic elections was severely compromised. In this uncertain transitional period, it was especially important that vulnerable populations be educated about their rights and responsibilities in the forthcoming elections and in the new political system. As its own limited response, the GBM launched its civic education program called the Movement for Free and Fair Elections.

The Movement for Free and Fair Elections was started in June 1992 by Wangari Maathai in conjunction with a few other people, including some who had been at the forefront of the agitation for political pluralism in Kenya in the late 1980s, such as Reverend Timothy Njoya, lawyer Paul Muite, and members of newly formed pressure groups such as Release Political Prisoners (RPP) and Mothers of Political Prisoners. The goal of the civic education campaign was to hold twenty-five seminars countrywide and to translate educational materials into local languages for wider dissemination across the country before the elections at the end of 1992. The initial seminar was held in Nyeri town in the central province of Kenya in June 1992. Thereafter, various seminars were held elsewhere, and by the time of the elections in December 1992, fifteen such seminars had been held, mostly in the central province and at least two in the western province.[16] Many other opportunities, such as the GBM annual general meeting in September 1992, were turned into mini Free and Fair seminar sessions. As part of my field research, I attended more than ten such seminars and occasionally traveled with Maathai to seminar venues. I was able to see the organizational work and constraints involved in the civic education program.

The Free and Fair seminars were usually held in church halls, where local residents assembled in the form of a town meeting to listen to various presentations by guest speakers, followed by an open forum where members of the public would ask questions and venture their own opinions regarding various issues. A typical seminar attracted between 300 and 700 participants from the local area. Calling on the expertise and experiences of notable individuals and professionals, including agitators for political pluralism, the Free and Fair seminars covered a variety of topics on the nature of the recent political transitions and the role citizens were required to play.

Typical seminar presentations included expositions on the depth of repression in the former single-party state and the necessity for the transition to political pluralism; the workings of a multiparty democracy and expectations for both the leaders and the voters, especially in terms of political participation and accountability; the importance of elections and requirements for voting in the approaching elections, as well as the way the winner (especially of the presidency) would be determined; and the need for safeguarding human rights, releasing political prisoners, and repealing repressive laws. Other seminar themes were related to recurrent problems in Kenya's political culture, such as idolizing politicians, the role of money in politics and especially elections, and corruption. (See a typical pamphlet reproduced in Appendix B.)

Few local leaders (especially those associated with the incumbent regime) attended the seminars, and in only one instance was a local administrative officer (a chief) visibly present. Much of the preparation for the seminars (such as securing the church halls and publicity) was undertaken by the local residents after contacting the GBM secretariat. The established GBM network of grassroots groups, with their easy access to local communities (including tree beneficiaries), was invaluable for the logistics of convening the seminars. Indeed, one of the resolutions passed by delegates attending the September 1992 general meeting expressed support for the civic education initiative, and members undertook to make arrangements to hold seminars in their areas. Once again, as with the green belt tree nurseries, the GBM did not impose a Free and Fair seminar on an area or group but insisted on being invited by the area residents, notably members of the local green belt group or groups.

The fear of the repressive state was not totally erased, however, even as the nation prepared for multiparty elections. In certain instances, the GBM had to reschedule seminars because of last-minute refusals by church leaders to allow seminars to take place in their compounds. In one telling case, a priest locked the church hall and left the compound, leaving word that the hall would be unavailable for the scheduled Free and Fair seminar. Similarly, the seminar organizers were subjected to harassment by state officials, especially the provincial administration. This was particularly the case outside the central province (that is, outside areas that were considered opposition strongholds), where they were stopped or intimidated by state agents.[17]

It should be pointed out that despite efforts to make the civic education program objective, it was overwhelmingly anti-KANU. This was not an accident. First, the GBM had had many run-ins with the KANU government in its work, including advocacy efforts, and had also suffered official harassment for its antigovernment stands, such as its support of Mothers of Political Prisoners or its close association with oppositional politics. Such state harassment was directed not at Maathai alone (who had been arrested and once beaten unconscious) but also against field-workers, who were hounded by the secret police, and against women's groups, which had been told "not to plant Wangari Maathai's trees" at the height of the Uhuru Park saga. Second, the people who helped organize the seminars and who were invited to give presentations and testimonials had been at the center of the agitation for multiparty democracy in Kenya, such as Paul Muite and Timothy Njoya—both vehement critics of the single-party KANU regime. Similarly, others included mothers of political prisoners who were still being held on charges of opposing the single-party state. More broadly, however, in much of the country, the tide was clearly against KANU—the architect of the single-party state and an unconvincing convert to political pluralism. Many therefore considered the multiparty polls as a prime opportunity to vote out the KANU regime (see *Society* [August–December 1992]).[18]

The Movement for Free and Fair Elections was also intimately linked to the Middle Ground Group (MGG), an ad hoc group of opposition activists whose main goal was to reunite the main opposition party FORD, which had spearheaded the campaign for political pluralism in 1990–91 but had split into two rival parties in mid-1992. With the split in FORD, the opposition to KANU was bound to lose the election and consequently endanger many political reforms and reformers.[19] Later, when efforts to unite the parties failed, the MGG vigorously pushed them to field a single presidential candidate against the incumbent, President Moi. This effort included public opinion polls in several areas, press conferences, and a campaign to collect petitions and signatures from the public. As the election date drew near, the MGG agenda became an integral part of the Free and Fair seminars. It would have been difficult to separate the two even if the organizers had wanted to, since the two efforts shared the same major participants who were committed to taking both messages to all corners of the republic.[20]

It is difficult to measure the impact of the GBM's Movement for Free and Fair Elections in the communities it reached. The numbers are not likely to be large—a couple of thousand at the most. Moreover, since these efforts were spread out over fifteen areas (which included many constituencies where registered voters numbered over 20,000), the effect may seem minimal and inconsequential. However, it is important to point out that the Free and Fair Movement was not an ambitious program to reach all voters nationwide but only as many as possible through the GBM's grassroots network of members and affiliated groups.

A few other groups were pursuing similar civic education campaigns, for example, the NCCK and the Catholic Secretariat. The Catholic Secretariat, through its Justice and Peace Commission, held seminars for its clergymen from dioceses across the country. They, in turn, passed the election education on to their local congregations. Similarly, the NCCK carried out its own civic education campaign, most notably in a series of posters, newspaper advertisements, and reports in the local dailies and through politicized sermons in many of its member churches. Apart from these efforts by church bodies, the GBM was the only development NGO pursuing a nationwide civic education program through its grassroots network of development activities. This reflects the GBM's broader commitment to advocacy for good governance not only of the environment but also in national politics.

The GBM and the Civil Society Thesis

The case of the GBM illustrates much of the received wisdom of the civil society–democratization thesis, but at the same time it raises some questions as to the efficacy of this proposition. As with Undugu, the GBM case illustrates the importance of successful "production" goals in facilitating a grassroots empowerment agenda (Elliot 1987; Fowler 1991b). In addition, it demonstrates the potential use of empowered clients as carriers of society's challenge against a repressive state. This is especially so when these clients act on their own (as with the Undugu kiosk owners) or become networks of mobilized constituencies through which the organization may pursue further agitation for a freer civil society. Thus, the evidence from the case studies clearly suggests that NGOs can contribute to grassroots empowerment through their productive ("modernization") goals. What is in doubt is whether NGOs acting as organizations or institutions are necessarily able or willing to agitate for political reform. The experience of these two similar NGOs suggests that even with comparable resources, mobilization capacities, and achieved grassroots empowerment, one organization can contribute to the expansion of opportunities in civil society, whereas the other is unable to do so.

The expectation that civil society organizations will contribute to democratization in Africa rests in large part on the understanding that these organizations represent alternative resources, organization, and mobilization that can be and have been brought to bear on authoritarian states to reform. Although the case of the Kenyan NGO Network successfully opposing controlling legislation supports and elaborates the factors behind this expectation, the cases of the two individual NGOs underscore two important variables. One is the dimension of political opportunity available at any given time, which largely determines the viability of political actions in civil society (see Chapter 3).The second is the actual *will* to take advantage of this political opportunity (and organizational resources and empowered grassroots networks) to pursue the goals of the democratization movement. As the case of the GBM suggests, this political will lies not in the institutional capacities of an NGO but in its leadership. This personality dimension is crucial and, I argue, largely explains the two faces of civil society. Undugu and the GBM are similar development organizations and had similar political opportunities, yet the former is largely indifferent to institutional possibilities of influencing state–civil society relations, whereas the latter exploits available resources and opportunities to challenge the state.

As pointed out earlier, for Undugu, the impasse stems from its thorough institutionalization, especially the oversight of a board constituted of persons connected with government, which enhances the NGO's programmatic objectives but is unlikely to approve explicit political actions. In contrast, the GBM is able to pursue more forthright political challenges against the state due to a lack of such institutionalization or, to put it more precisely and more positively, due to the unfettered personal drive of Wangari Maathai, its founder and coordinator. The political decision to use available resources to challenge the undemocratic state is one that no particular type of organization is predisposed to make merely because of its institutional resources, organization, or voice; such a decision is made because of the personal initiative of its leadership.

Indeed, the fact that Ezra Mbogori, as director of the Undugu Society, also led the NGO Network in challenging the NGO Coordination Act (see Chapter 3) only emphasizes the political stasis in Undugu as an organization and the importance of NGO heads as political actors. In this case, it was Mbogori rather than Undugu who contributed to the NGO Network being at the "cutting edge" of the battle to establish a freer civil society in Kenya (Diamond, Linz, and Lipset 1988). Similarly, the experience of the GBM elaborated in this chapter suggests the centrality of Maathai in all aspects of her organization and especially in its politicization and its political work. The centrality of Maathai's leadership to the GBM's mission in civil society underscores the view that without her, there would most likely be no Green Belt Movement as it is known today and almost surely none of the contributions to state–civil society relations outlined in this chapter.

Notes

1. An oft-repeated accusation against the Green Belt Movement by the Kenyan government is that the GBM has no trees to show for its "long and loud" existence. See, for example, debates during the Uhuru Park saga, *Daily Nation*, November 9–24, 1989.
2. As with the discussion on the Undugu Society of Kenya (Chapter 4), the

historical discussion on the Green Belt Movement is based on information gleaned from extensive archival research at GBM offices. Most of the documents consulted were internal reports, including periodic field reports, as well as documents related to NORAD and NOVIB, two of the GBM's major donors. Other information comes from interviews conducted in 1992–93 with Wangari Maathai, Nyaguthii Chege, and Njogu Kahare.

3. The NCWK was founded in 1964 as an umbrella organization for national and local women's groups.

4. Green Belt International has its headquarters in San Francisco, California, but is dormant. The PAGBM was launched in November 1986 through seminars for the purpose of providing training and practical experience to persons and groups interested in forming GBMs in their own countries. The initial seminar was sponsored by UNEP and the African Development Fund. Three seminars have been held so far in 1986, 1987, and 1993. The countries represented are Tanzania, Somalia, Sudan, Ethiopia, Zimbabwe, Burundi, Uganda, Swaziland, Zambia, Malawi, and Lesotho.

5. In many training seminars I attended and on field visits, I went through the motions of the ten important steps in the GBM procedures, including filling out forms with grassroots members. See GBM [1990] for complete details on the forms and procedures.

6. The U.S. dollar equivalent is approximated by converting at the 1992–93 exchange rate of K Sh 65 to the dollar throughout this chapter.

7. The GBM estimates that voluntary professional (administrative and training) and grassroots labor constitutes over K Sh 1 million (US$15,000) or over 20 percent of the annual budget (Mbaya 1993).

8. Kenya broke off diplomatic relations with Norway following acrimony between the two countries over the kidnap and arrest of a former member of parliament (Koigi wa Wamwere) at the Kenya-Uganda border town of Busia by the Kenyan government. Wamwere, who was visiting Uganda, had been granted political asylum in Norway (*Weekly Review*, October 26, 1990, 5–7).

9. Based on a physical count of surviving trees planted by the GBM up to 1986.

10. These figures cover only a few of the twenty-seven districts of operations, since the NORAD and NOVIB grants to the GBM cover the campaign in specific districts.

11. This is a small average, given that during my field visits, I counted over 900 surviving trees (excluding fruit and exotic trees) that had been issued by a single tree nursery to one farmer in one season. One nursery I visited had issued over 30,000 seedlings in the previous twelve months but had been paid for only a fraction—a recurrent problem due to poor record-keeping. It is therefore possible that the average number of surviving trees may be larger than this estimate and thus provide a larger income for the women's groups.

12. See note 4 above.

13. This critique was constructed by participants of the 1993 Pan-African Green Belt Movement (PAGBM) seminar in Nairobi and is based on an example of environmentally destructive development from Uganda.

Reproduced from personal notes.

14. Though it is the official and legal gazette, the *Kenya Gazette* is an obscure outlet for policy pronouncements that are likely to affect so many citizens.

15. *Maendeleo* vilified Maathai and the Green Belt Movement in staged countrywide demonstrations during the Uhuru Park saga and at the height of the multiparty debate.

16. Most of the Free and Fair seminars were held in the central province, which is one of the opposition strongholds. There, the KANU government knew that the tide was already against it, so it was possible to hold the seminars more freely than in those areas where KANU was counting on swing votes, such as in the western and rift valley provinces. In these provinces, the Free and Fair seminars and the seminar leaders were subjected to official harassment, such as being stopped by the police or having seminars canceled. For instance, in the rift valley province, which KANU stalwarts declared a "KANU zone," Maathai was "forbidden" from setting foot in the province by a prominent KANU politician.

17. See note 16 above.

18. Even though KANU eventually won the election, it was by a small margin, and the vote was overwhelmingly in favor of the opposition parties—split three ways though (see Barkan 1993).

19. As the then U.S. ambassador to Kenya admonished the opposition, "If they do not hang together now, they would surely hang separately after the elections" (personal communication from opposition party activist; original citation unknown).

20. I focus only on the civic education campaign rather than the more partisan MGG effort because the former more than the latter sought to impart democratic values and orientations to further democratization at the grassroots. This does not mean that the more partisan effort by the MGG did not contribute to the democratization process.

6

NGOs, Civil Society, and Democratization

IN ORDER TO DRAW OUT THE LESSONS from the empirical evidence presented in the preceding chapters, it is useful to recall some of the issues mentioned in Chapter 1. First, what does the empirical evidence indicate about NGOs' contribution to democratization in Africa? Second, what factors explain the direct challenges to undemocratic states by some NGOs and, conversely, the lack of challenge from others? Third, what implications do the preceding case studies have for the thesis that civil society will contribute positively to democratization in Africa? The analysis presented in this book confirms some of the central arguments advanced by civil society optimists, suggests some necessary distinctions and specifications regarding the present understanding and, finally, raises some fundamental questions regarding civil society's promise of democratization.

Underscoring Political Opportunity

What does the empirical evidence indicate about civil society's contribution to democratization? At face value, the experience of the Kenyan NGO community collectively challenging the NGO legislation introduced by the government in 1990 reaffirms the vision of civil society as directly engaged in actions to force political change in African countries. As this particular case shows, NGOs were organized, resourceful, and conscious actors contributing to the political reform movement in Kenya. This experience therefore underscores what most analysts have argued is the potential of civil society organizations to contribute to political reform (Bratton 1989a; Diamond, Linz, and Lipset 1988; Chazan 1992; Harbeson, Rothchild, and Chazan 1994). In this instance, NGOs were clearly acting as a "bulwark"

(Barkan, McNulty, and Ayeni 1991) against state repression and were at "the cutting edge" (Diamond, Linz, and Lipset 1988) of forcing political reform from within civil society.

Without essentially disagreeing with the above conclusion, I treat civil society actions as the *dependent* variables that need to be explained rather than as the causal variables of political reform. This perspective leads to a quest for factors that explain civil society's recent efficacy in challenging the state in Africa. The case of the NGO community in Kenya suggests that collective organization, increased resources, and alliances with other influential actors in society are necessary for credible action against the state. Another crucial contributing factor is the availability of political opportunity, which, according to Sidney Tarrow (1991), reduces the risk involved in revolting. In Kenya, institutional access to the state opened up in 1990, especially as the single-party sought to respond to mounting criticism of its governance structures. The opportunity for the NGO Network to agitate was clearly indicated by the degree to which state elites were willing to listen to and negotiate with NGOs—something that had been very unlikely prior to 1990, when the single party was the unchallenged power over state and society.[1]

Importantly, the case of NGOs in Kenya highlights that, as a community (and a fairly central component of organized [civil] society in Kenya), NGOs were not predisposed to oppose the single-party dictatorship until their very existence and free operation were threatened by the NGO Coordination Act of 1990. It was a self-interested survivalist instinct that propelled NGOs to oppose the state, and only in the specific area of legislation concerning their operations. Indeed, it was not until later, when the democratic movement was well under way (after the legalization of opposition parties), that the NGO community became a recognizable component of the spectrum of organizations challenging the single-party state to reform. The collective NGO action against the state was therefore a result of the threat of restrictive legislation rather than of an articulated consciousness to oppose the repressive state and to promote democratic values. Civil society is evidently not necessarily predisposed to challenging and democratizing the African state (Bayart 1986, 1993; Gyimah-Boadi 1994; Callaghy 1994).

In addition to exposing the "two faces" of civil society, the case studies suggest that NGOs have not always been opposed to the state. The case of the Undugu Society shows how closely some organizations in civil society work with the state; the Green Belt Movement (GBM), in contrast, illustrates the change in these relations over time. The evolution of the NGO Network's challenge against the NGO

Coordination Act clearly shows the importance of an emerging political opportunity allowing NGOs to pursue opposition actions at lower risk. The necessity for political opportunity, which is evident in the actions of NGOs in Kenya, underscores that civil society activity does not cause political liberalization, but that the democratic movement is a larger force engulfing the whole of society to which civil society actors respond. Even though NGOs occupy an influential position in civil society, command considerable resources and voice, and have leverage against developing states such as Kenya, they are not the originators of reform movements. Indeed, they are respondents to both the repressive capacities of the state and the reformist backlash against the state from sectors of civil society (most prominently, from displaced elites). The resurgence of civil society and its political activity in Africa therefore reflects a social movement of which it may be only a belated but nevertheless significant sign.

Once we admit the importance of political opportunity to the success of civil society's oppositional actions, one question remains: what differentiates (a) civil society organizations (such as the NGO Network) that are resourceful, organized, and able to ensure their own survival, or those (such as individual NGOs) that are able and willing to pursue broader goals of fundamentally altering political structures, and (b) those that are similarly endowed but are unable or unwilling to pursue such forthright political actions in opposition to the state? The case studies of the two NGOs in Kenya underscore that institutional resources, including political opportunity, are necessary but not sufficient to enable organizations in civil society to contribute directly to the pressure for political change. The explanation for the two faces of civil society lies in the willingness of the leadership of these organizations to use organizational resources against the repressive state. For NGOs, this means turning the leverage drawn from coveted development resources, mobilizational capacities, and institutional access to international, national, and local actors (for example, aid donors, lobbying points, and grassroots networks) to the effort of undermining the monolithic state. This political will stems from a fairly arbitrary element of personal leadership within civil society organizations.

NGO Elites and Personal Rule

The theoretical literature on civil society and democratization in Africa is silent on the role of elites in civil society's opposition to the state. It is important to bear in mind that many of the civil society organizations that have been involved in opposing the state had previously been docile political actors. For instance, organizations that have been at the forefront of opposing the Moi regime, such as the National Council of Churches of Kenya, the GBM, and the Law Society of Kenya, all had amicable relations with the KANU government prior to the late 1980s. One cannot assert convincingly that these organizations have institutionalized the oppositional dynamic merely because they are part of civil society. Indeed, the persons leading these organizations are most identifiable with the opposition movement, whereas the organizations themselves provide resourceful platforms to propel diverse political agendas.[2] For example, as its chairmanship changed hands, the Law Society of Kenya switched back and forth from confronting the increasingly authoritarian state in Kenya to supporting it in the 1980s. In 1989–90, the Law Society's chairmanship became the subject of intense electoral competition and court injunctions as two factions fought for control of the association. One faction was supportive of and supported by the Moi regime, and the other was avowedly opposed to the KANU dictatorship.[3] For each faction, the offices of the Law Society of Kenya would have provided a platform to advance its own interests. Similarly, the NCCK reached the zenith of its activism under the leadership of Reverend Samuel Kobia but took a decidedly more passive stance following the election of Reverend Mutava Musyimi as secretary-general in 1993.

The importance of personal leadership in the political actions of organizations in civil society is clearly evident in the case of the GBM; it is similarly underscored in the case of the Undugu Society precisely because of the *absence* of organizational political action resulting from a lack of personal political direction by the leadership. As I argued earlier, the institutionalization in Undugu and its close association with establishment figures (see Appendix A) has diminished the possibility of direct political action by the organization. Ezra Mbogori's leading role in the NGO Network's opposition to the state is suggestive of his own personal commitment to the reform movement. However, the organization he led (Undugu), because of its institutionalization, does not lend itself to personal political direction. It is evident from comparing Undugu and the GBM that institutionalization (at least the kind that has occurred in Undugu) may undermine an organization's ability to pursue political engagements. The personal leadership provided by Wangari Maathai in a nonbureaucratic organization is what gave the GBM much of its drive in opposing the single-party state.

The case of the Central Organization of Trade Unions (COTU), the national umbrella body of trade unions in Kenya—an indisputable civil society member—provides an additional example of the role played by leaders in determining the political direction taken by civil society organizations. In the run-up to the December 1992 elections, the leadership of COTU, which had in 1990 been officially annexed to the single party, was a strong supporter of the KANU government. (This is itself an indication of reactionary forces in civil society.) However, shortly after the elections, COTU's secretary-general Joseph Mugalla fell out with the KANU leadership, ostensibly because Moi's cabinet appointments sidelined Mugalla's cronies or patrons and caused the fortunes of a few politicians from Mugalla's Luhya ethnic group to plummet (*Weekly Review,* May 7, 1993, 11–12). For the first time in years, COTU lamented the implementation of the economic structural adjustment program, which, among other things, had eroded workers' purchasing power. The national union therefore demanded a general wage increase to compensate workers and threatened a nationwide strike if this was not granted; this agitation led to President Moi's missing the Labor Day celebrations for the first time in his presidency and a haphazard one-day general strike.[4] Soon thereafter, COTU was plagued by leadership wrangles that culminated in premature elections that forced the incumbents out. The KANU government's hand in this "coup" was most manifest in police interference in the voting (for instance, in restricting members' access to the voting hall). The new leadership of the trade union movement was once again strongly pro-KANU and proceeded to retract the demand for a general wage increase.

Where does the trade union movement in Kenya belong—among progressive forces for democratization, or among reactionary forces for the dominant former single party? This depends very much on the direction that the labor elites choose. Despite the resources at the disposal of the union and its affiliate branches, especially its mobilization capacities, COTU has not contributed to the strength of progressive forces in civil society in Kenya. The progressive tendencies of some civil society organizations should therefore not mislead analysts into thinking that such organizations are naturally predisposed to democratic government or that all of civil society is progressive. Rather, it is the (sometimes whimsical, often unaccountable) sway of the leadership that directs the political actions of civil society organizations, especially when decision making has yet to be institutionalized or democratized. Herein lies the contradiction of civil society in its effort to democratize African states.

The fact that the organizational actions of NGOs and other actors in civil society are a product of personal direction by elites occupying resourceful societal institutions is, in a fundamental sense, no different from what Jackson and Rosberg (1982) describe as the organization of *state* power through "personal rule" in sub-Saharan Africa. It is especially evident in opposition parties and in organizations that have been leading agitators for democratic reform. For instance, the following personalities heading or associated with important civil associational bodies are recognized as important political entities independent of their organizations: Paul Muite, the former chairman of the Law Society of Kenya who is credited with catapulting it to political prominence; Reverend Timothy Njoya of the Presbyterian Church of East Africa; Reverend Samuel Kobia of the NCCK; and Bishop Henry Okullu of the Catholic Church.

The centrality of personal politics within the reform movement has been most evident in the main opposition parties. The founder-leaders of such parties, much like the founding fathers of African nations, have acted largely above the institution of party, and when institutional processes (such as party elections) have threatened their dominance, they have circumvented such rules (for example, by changing election codes). When a party like the Forum for the Restoration of Democracy (FORD) could not accommodate more than one personal ruler, it split into rival parties.[5] The centrality of "personal rule" (Jackson and Rosberg 1982) in civil society and especially in its oppositional undertakings against the repressive state undermines civil society's promise of democratic development because it does not offer a revision of existing power relations in the state and in society.

Grassroots Empowerment as a Path to Democracy

As analysts of democratic change in Africa, students of civil society are concerned with the reorganization of power relations in African states. The civil society thesis—that civil society actors are important contributors to democratic change—is essentially a statement on their positive contribution to altering power relations in Africa. Analysts therefore need to raise fundamental questions regarding where civil society actors derive their power to oppose the state and, even more importantly, where this power resides. Does it, for instance, derive from grassroots mobilization and participation? Does it reside with citizens at the local level or in representative and accountable elites? If one can conclusively answer these questions in the affirmative, then civil society can be said to hold the promise of democratizing African states.

Labour Unions

Much of the discussion of the civil society thesis as well as the empirical evidence presented here assumes the dominant view of civil society as an organizational arena (Stepan 1988; Bratton 1989a). What I have demonstrated in the case studies is that the organizational contributions of civil society to political reform are much more nuanced than many studies of activist organizations would lead us to believe. More importantly, when organizations have embarked on a conscious effort to agitate for reform, their actions have depended on external factors that are favorable to their pursuits in the short term. For instance, in the case of the NGO Network, it is evident that NGO leverage vis-à-vis the state was enhanced by externally controlled factors, that is, increased development aid and external support for political reform. However, the flow of development resources is never assured, especially since the increased resources can be attributed to a prevailing lack of confidence in the accountability of the state, which has forced donors to look elsewhere for more sound development administration. Does this mean that once the state's accountability is restored, development funds may flow there again, thus detracting from civil society's current leverage? Does this mean that when the current wave of mobilization fizzles out, civil society, left with little opportunity for independent political action, will cease to hold the state to account?

One level of civil society action that has largely been ignored but that may lead to more durable changes in African political life is grassroots empowerment. Both the Green Belt Movement and the Undugu Society of Kenya show that grassroots empowerment is an important outgrowth of fairly mundane development activities that require no explicit commitment by the NGO to oppose the state. It is evident in either case that NGO activities aimed at enhancing the social and economic capacities of local communities and exposing them to interactions with the state enable these communities to act on their own. The case of the twenty women from the Undugu Society who protested and sought compensation from the government over the demolition of their businesses is an example. In this case, the women acted to challenge the state in spite of the lack of involvement (or extra resources and leverage) of their "civil society" organization. The involvement of rural women in the GBM's civic education campaign is similarly illustrative of their willingness to participate directly in the democratic political process. The GBM's own commitment to grassroots voter education to facilitate independent political action is itself an indication of its leadership's recognition of the peril of relying only on organizational agitation facilitated by external factors.

Implications for the Civil Society Promise

In examining the civil society thesis, this book has looked at both the organizational actions of NGOs opposing the state and their mundane development actions in grassroots communities. Simply as organizational actors vis-à-vis the state, NGOs are unevenly supportive of the civil society thesis. NGO *organizational* power, as is evident throughout the preceding chapters, derives from increased development resources (which is heavily dependent on external influences) and resides primarily in the NGO leadership. The choice of whether to turn this organizational power to oppose a repressive state is solely in the hands of organizational elites. Both of these factors limit the possibility of NGOs acting as a permanent bulwark against the state or altering fundamental power relations in African countries.

Are civil society institutions merely the organized part of society and manifestations of entrenched social interests and cleavages, or do they in fact contain the requisite consciousness to pursue, practice, and preserve democracy? This study demonstrates that civil society as the organized part of society has the potential to challenge the state, but this is uneven and by no means an assured predisposition. At the same time, civil society is not immune to the normal politics propelled by or viewed through variables such as ethnicity, class, and so forth. For instance, a casual survey of the leadership of the opposition against the former single-party state in Kenya (be it in civil society or among defecting state elites) reveals a concentration of elites from the Kikuyu and Luo groups. Although no objective studies have been carried out, there is a shared impression among NGO observers (and the government) that the nonstate development agencies have come to be dominated by central province (essentially Kikuyu) elites and intelligentsia. To the KANU government, these organizations (along with the mainline Protestant churches) represent entrenched ethnic interests. The fact that these organizations currently champion democratic governance may reflect the attempts of displaced elites to regain access to state power. The potential or demonstrated abilities of civil society organizations to pursue democratizing actions must therefore be examined in the context of the broader politics of any state, and assumptions regarding their uniqueness or immunity to usual political proclivities must be abandoned.

Whether the political actions of civil society organizations articulate the demands of their grassroots memberships is difficult to discern. The major oppositional undertakings of organizations such as the GBM do not include any direct action by grassroots members. For instance, the GBM's successful opposition against government plans to build a sixty-story structure in a public park in Nairobi did not necessitate mobilization of its rural women's groups. Similarly, Undugu's distance from the political actions of its clients suggests that the NGO was not acting as an intermediary representing the political demands of disempowered communities. Given the evidence in the preceding chapters, it is a mistake for analysts to view civil society organizations as steadfast supporters of democratization. The only interests that such organizations are likely to represent forcefully are those that are intimately tied to their own organizational existence. The case of the NGO Network illustrates this well. Grassroots empowerment through NGO development activities is crucial, however. This is where civil society's promise of contributing to democratic development in Africa should be rooted. In particular, as the example of independent political action by members of the Undugu Society illustrates, grassroots empowerment is possible even when the organization itself remains aloof toward direct political engagements. Moreover, grassroots empowerment presents the possibility of civil society organizations not only contributing to the immediate reform process but also enabling local communities to participate in and preserve evolving democratic political processes.

The possibilities for citizen empowerment that are evident in the cases of the Undugu Society and the GBM are especially attractive, given the uncertainty of the transition to multiparty politics in Kenya and elsewhere in Africa. Even without explicit political maneuvers, NGOs are well placed to further democratization through grassroots empowerment within their development activities. Through projects that enhance the political capacities of local communities—from mundane socioeconomic projects to more political undertakings, such as civic education campaigns—NGOs may be able to mobilize citizens and influence the direction of political change toward greater participatory democracy and accountable government in Africa.

Notes

1. Tarrow (1991) also considers times when political alignments are in flux and when the ruling class is divided as opportune moments for revolt. Both of these were evident in the increased number of defections from the single-party KANU and the formation of new opposition parties by prominent politicians after the government legalized opposition parties in November 1991.

2. The leadership is also predominantly Kikuyu—the previously dominant ethnic group during the Kenyatta regime (1963–78) that has steadily been displaced by Moi in coalition with other minority groups. Ethnic competition may therefore extenuate state-society tensions, but it may also be partly responsible for the differences in civil society responses to the state. For instance, both *Maendeleo ya Wanawake* and COTU were led by leaders from the western province Luhya group, an ethnic group whose prominent politicians were recognizably backing Moi and KANU (*Weekly Review,* May 7, 1993). Not surprisingly, these organizations supported KANU.

3. See *Weekly Review,* April 6, 1990, pp. 19–20; April 16, 1990, p. 16; June 1, 1990, pp. 4–8; June 29, 1990, pp. 25–26; August 10, 1990, pp. 16–18.

4. On previous government involvement in COTU affairs, see *Weekly Review,* November 14, 1986, pp. 12–14; May 23, 1986, pp. 3–5. On Mugalla's sudden change against the KANU establishment, see *Weekly Review,* March 28, 1993, pp. 14–16; April 16, 1993, pp. 22–23; April 30, 1993, pp. 10–11; May 7, 1993, pp. 3–12; June 4, 1993, p. 18. On Mugalla's fate after leading COTU to confrontation, see *Weekly Review,* August 6, 1993, pp. 12–13.

5. The splintering of the main opposition party FORD and the proliferation of numerous smaller parties formed and dominated by prominent personalities are illustrative. For accounts of these developments, see the elaborate daily coverage in *Daily Nation* (August–October 1992) or the more analytical if biased accounts in *Weekly Review* or *Society* (various issues, August–October 1992).

Appendix A
Undugu Society of Kenya

Board of Directors of the Undugu Society of Kenya

Fr. Arnold Grol, chair and founder
Mrs. A. B. N. Wandera, vice-chair and former Ministry of Culture and
    Social Services official
Mr. J. E. Onyango, treasurer
Mr. Ezra Mbogori, secretary and executive director
Mr. Arthur Buluma, member
Mr. Kiraithe O. A. Nyaga, member
Prof. H. S. K. Mwaniki, member
Mr. R. C. Makokha, member
Rev. Samuel Kobia, member and NCCK secretary-general
Mr. Fabio Dallape, member and former executive director
Mr. Harold Miller, member

Board of Trustees of the Undugu Society of Kenya

Fr. Arnold Grol, founder
Hon. P. H. Okondo, former cabinet minister
Sr. Edel Bahati
Justice Effie Owuor, High Court judge
Dr. Joseph Odhiambo
Hon. Amos Wako, attorney general of Kenya

Donors to Undugu (1990–91)

Terre des Hommes
Undugu Friends Circle—Germany
NACHU/REDSO

Kindernothilfe
Undugu Friends Circle—Holland
UNICEF—Kenya

(cont.)

Source: USK 1992.

Save the Children—Canada
O. E. D. Austria
Hofstee Stichting
TROCAIRE
ADV Landesregierung (Austria)
GTZ/GATE
Norwegian Housewives Association
Partnership Africa Canada
Terra Nuova
National Fund for the Disabled, Kenya

Caritas Netherlands
Ford Foundation
CEBEMO
Intermediate Technology
    Development Group
Community Development
    International
SNV
Norwegian Church Aid/NORAD
CAFOD

Undugu's Departments and Program Activities

Department	Functions and Activities
Community Organization *gardens trees*	Mobilizes communities and facilitates group formation and functioning
Low-Cost Housing	Provides improved and affordable housing in slum communities
Community Health Program	Provides health education and counseling for communities; new main focus: AIDS
Business Development Unit	Provides business advice and credit to groups and individuals in slums
Export Unit *Herbs, medicines*	Exports and markets items made by women's groups in USK programs
Urban Agriculture and Appropriate Technologies	Experiments with agriculture in slum community land for food security
Katangi Agricultural Program	Conducts agricultural experiments in a semiarid area outside Nairobi (it is from such unproductive land that slum dwellers originally flee)
Mathare Valley Program	Consists of an integrated development program
Kibera Program	Consists of an integrated development program
Kitui-Pumwani Program	Consists of an integrated development program (cont.)

Department	Functions and Activities
Street Girls Program	Provides education, counseling, and rehabilitation for street girls, including commercial sex workers
Parking Boys Program	Provides education, counseling, and rehabilitation for street boys
Undugu Basic Education Program (UBEP)	Provides nonformal education to street and slum children
Machuma Schools	Provides basic, nonformal education for street children who do not have time for full-time UBEP participation (most of them sell *machuma* [scrap metal])
Sponsorship Program	Provides sponsorships for slum children unable to pay school fees
Program for the Handicapped	Targets handicapped in the slums for better integration into schools
Informal-Sector Program	Provides skill training for informal-sector production for UBEP graduates and other street children
Motor Vehicle/Mechanic Unit	Maintains USK vehicles and offers commercial repair services to the public
Industrial Design Unit	Designs products (for example, furniture) for USK production units
Administrative Support	Includes the information office, providing administrative support

Energy
water
Transport

Appendix B
The Green Belt Movement

Sample Pamphlet from the Movement for Free and Fair Elections

The Movement for Free and Fair Elections

The Movement for Free and Fair Elections will provide space for the people to create a just, peaceful and democratic society. Kenyans will liberate themselves rather than wait to be liberated. They will decide to be morally just, upright, truthful and humane. They will shed fear, apathy and cynicism. They will pick representatives of their choice. They will not allow self-appointed, imposed or co-opted collaborators. To achieve this the people should do the following:

1. Enhance the campaign for the release of all political prisoners who have been denied their constitutional right to register and vote.

   Koigi wa Wamwere, Rumba Kinuthia, and *Mirugi Kariuki* were discriminated against during the State's *nolle prosequi* entered in respect of other co-accused because they are political giants in Nakuru district [which was declared a KANU zone in the period preceding the politically motivated tribal clashes in the Rift Valley province].

2. Encourage all eligible voters to register.

3. Assist those who need assistance throughout the entire electoral process to prevent them being cheated or misled.

4. Engage in discussions for the purpose of educating each other about the electoral process.

5. Expose electoral malpractices to the public and relevant officers without fear and despite efforts to intimidate.

Source: GBM 1992b.

6. Do not surrender your birth right (i.e. your vote) like the biblical Esau and remember that the money they are dishing out has been stolen from coffee, tea, milk, licensing, sugar cane, road tolls, fees, charges, etc. They have used the same money to pay mercenaries to kill your people.

7. Identify and support candidates of your choice. Ensure that such candidates are elected freely and fairly irrespective of their political party.

8. Know that the candidates voted for do not belong to your political party. Rather, elect the best persons for the seventh Parliament which should create justice, peace and democratic institutions of governance.

9. Elect leaders who have demonstrated a commitment to the following qualities:
   - Human dignity
   - Justice
   - Concern for the poor
   - Moral principles (righteousness, integrity)
   - Incorruptibility
   - Courage
   - Mental acumen (accuracy and quickness of judgement)
   - Competence
   - Proper management of public funds and other national resources
   - Democratic governance

10. We shall not allow the greedy and the blood-thirsty to destroy our country. We are united and we shall have free and fair elections because we stand our ground and will not be moved. *Join the Movement for Free and Fair Elections and be an active participant in the first democratic election in thirty years!*

—Prof. Wangari Maathai
For and on Behalf of the F & F Movement

Main Donors to the Green Belt Movement

UNDP
Danish Children Project
Norwegian Forestry Project
NOVIB
NORAD
Finland Coalition
Various other smaller foundations and private individuals

References

African NGOs Self-Reliance and Development Advocacy Group (ASDAG). 1991. "A Code of Practice for the NGO Sector in Africa." Addis Ababa, October.

Allen, Jeffrey R. 1992. "The Green Belt Movement: The Roots of Its Success." In *Readings on Environmental Issues in Kenya: Papers on Environment and Development*, ed. Jack Shepherd. Papers by participants in the Dartmouth College 1992 Kenya Environmental Foreign Study Program, Hanover, N.H.

Amis, Philip H. 1983. "A Shanty Town of Tenants: The Commercialization of Unauthorized Housing in Nairobi." Ph.D. thesis, University of Kent.

Antrobus, Peggy. 1987. "Funding for NGOs: Issues and Options." *World Development* 15 (autumn suppl.): 95–102.

Azarya, Victor. 1988. "Re-ordering State-Society Relations: Incorporation and Disengagement." In *Precarious Balance: State and Society in Africa*, ed. Donald Rothchild and Naomi Chazan. Boulder, Colo.: Westview.

Barkan, Joel D. 1992. "The Rise and Fall of a Governance Realm in Kenya." In *Governance and Politics in Africa*, ed. Goran Hyden and Michael Bratton. Boulder, Colo.: Lynne Rienner.

Barkan, Joel D. 1993. "Kenya: Lessons of a Flawed Election." *Journal of Democracy* 4(3): 85–99.

Barkan, Joel D., and Michael Chege. 1989. "Decentralizing the State: District Focus and the Politics of Reallocation in Kenya." *Journal of Modern African Studies* 27(3): 431–53.

Barkan, Joel D., Michael McNulty, and M. A. Ayeni. 1991. "'Hometown' Voluntary Associations, Local Development and the Emergence of Civil Society in Western Nigeria." *Journal of Modern African Studies* 29(3): 457–80.

Bayart, Jean-Francois. 1986. "Civil Society in Africa." In *Political Domination in Africa*, ed. Patrick Chabal. New York: Cambridge University Press.

Bayart, Jean-Francois. 1993. *The State in Africa: The Politics of the Belly*. New York: Longman.

Best, John, and David Brown. 1990. *AERDD Bulletin: NGOs in Development* (theme issue) 28 (February). University of Reading, Agricultural Extension and Rural Development Department.

Bratton, Michael. 1989a. "Beyond the State: Civil Society and Associational Life in Africa." *World Politics* 41(3): 407–30.

Bratton, Michael. 1989b. "The Politics of Government-NGO Relations in Africa." *World Development* 17(4): 569–87.

Bratton, Michael. 1994. "Civil Society and Political Transitions in Africa." In *Civil Society and the State in Africa*, ed. John W. Harbeson, Donald Rothchild, and Naomi Chazan. Boulder, Colo.: Lynne Rienner.

Brodhead, Tim. 1987. "NGOs: In One Year, Out the Other." *World Development* 15 (autumn suppl.): 1–6.

Brown, L. David, and David C. Korten. 1989. "The Role of Voluntary Organizations in Development." Concept paper prepared for the World Bank. Boston: Institute for Development Research.

Buiys, Pieter. 1984. "USK Briefing Paper on Financial Affairs." Financial Advisor's Report to USK Consultative Committee. Nairobi: USK.

Buturo, James. 1994. "NGOs, Democracy and Sustainable Development in Africa." *Voices from Africa* 5 (June): 29–36.

Callaghy, Thomas M. 1994. "Civil Society, Democracy, and Economic Change in Africa: A Dissenting Opinion about Resurgent Societies." In *Civil Society and the State in Africa*, ed. John W. Harbeson, Donald Rothchild, and Naomi Chazan. Boulder, Colo.: Lynne Rienner.

Chabal, Patrick, ed. 1986. *Political Domination in Africa: Reflections on the Limits of Power*. New York: Cambridge University Press.

Chazan, Naomi. 1992. "Africa's Democratic Challenge." *World Policy Journal* 9 (spring): 279–307.

Clark, John. 1990. *Democratizing Development: The Role of Voluntary Organizations*. West Hartford, Conn.: Kumarian Press.

Coninck, John de. 1992. *Evaluating the Impact of NGOs in Rural Poverty Alleviation: Uganda Case Study*. London: Overseas Development Institute.

Cowley, Deborah. 1987. "The Miracle Worker of Nairobi's Slums." *Reader's Digest* (October): 145–51.

Dahl, Robert. 1971. *Polyarchy: Participation and Opposition*. New Haven, Conn.: Yale University Press.

Daily Nation. Nairobi: Nation Newspapers.

Dallape, Fabio. n.d. "Role and Philosophy of USK towards Urban Squatter Settlement." Nairobi: USK.

Diamond, Larry, Juan Linz, and Seymour M. Lipset, eds. 1988. *Democracy in Developing Countries*. Vol. 2, *Africa*. Boulder, Colo.: Lynne Rienner.

Drabek, Anne Gordon, ed. 1987. *Development Alternatives: The Challenge for NGOs*. *World Development* 15 (autumn suppl.).

Eisinger, Peter K. 1973. "The Conditions of Protest Behavior in American Cities." *American Political Science Review* 67: 11–28.

Ekeh, Peter P. 1992. "The Constitution of Civil Society in African History and Politics." In *Proceedings of the Symposium on Democratic Transition in Africa, Ibadan, June 16–19, 1992*, ed. B. Caron, A. Gboyega, and E. Osaghae. CREDU Documents in Social Sciences and the Humanities.

Elliot, Charles. 1987. "Some Aspects of Relations between the North and South in the NGO Sector." *World Development* 15 (autumn suppl.): 57–68.

Engelstad, Sam. 1989. *Reflections on NGOs, the Bank and the Environment in Africa*. World Bank Divisional Publications Note no. 2. Washington, D.C.: World Bank.

Fowler, Alan. 1988. "New Scrambles in Africa." Paper presented at the East Africa-NOVIB Partners Seminar.

Fowler, Alan. 1989. "Non-Governmental Organizations and Development in Kenya: Interim Results of a Survey." Paper prepared for the workshop "Into the Nineties: NGOs during the Current Development Plan and Beyond," Institute for Development Studies, University of Nairobi, and KNCSS, Nairobi, August 14–16.

Fowler, Alan. 1991a. "Aide Memoir: NGO Legislation in Kenya." February 18.

Fowler, Alan. 1991b. "The Role of NGOs in Changing State-Society Relations: Perspectives from Eastern and Southern Africa" *Development Policy Review* 9(1): 53–84.

French, Mary Ann. 1992. "The Woman and Mother Earth." *Washington Post*, June 2, 1992, pp. D1–2.

GBM. [1990]. *The Green Belt Movement (Manual)*. Nairobi: GBM.

GBM. 1992a. "Educational Seminars Organized by the Movement for Free and Fair Elections in Conjunction with Middle Ground Group (MGG)." Nairobi: GBM.

GBM. 1992b. "Free and Fair Elections." Nairobi: GBM.

GBM. 1992c. "Gîkûndi Gia Gûtabarîra Gîthurano Kigaciru na Kîama." (Movement for Free and Fair Elections). Kikuyu translation. Nairobi: GBM.

GBM. 1992d. "Gîkûndi Gia Kûnyitithania Andû a Upinzani" (Middle Ground Group). Kikuyu translation. Nairobi: GBM.

GBM. 1992e. "Kutoka Kwa Kikundi cha Katikati (MGG) Washa ya Kuelimisha" (From the Middle Ground Group Education Section). Swahili translation. Nairobi: GBM.

GBM. n.d.a. *The Constitution of the Green Belt Movement*. Nairobi: GBM.

GBM. n.d.b. "The Green Belt Movement." Nairobi: GBM.

Gibbon, Peter. 1993. "'Civil Society' and Political Change, with Special Reference to 'Developmentalist' States." Paper presented at workshop "Experiences of Political Liberalization in Africa," Center for Development Research, Copenhagen, June 3–4.

Gitonga, Stephen Waigwa. 1992. "The Green Belt Movement Evaluation and Survey Report." Commissioned by GBM. Nairobi: GBM.

Goldstone, Jack A. 1980. "The Weakness of Organization: A New Look at Gamson's *The Strategy of Social Protest.*" *American Journal of Sociology* 85: 1017–42.

Grol, Father Arnold. 1992. "Reaching the Hard to Reach." Paper presented at a seminar on street children, Nairobi, September 2–4.

Grol, Father Arnold. n.d. "Some Casual Reflections about my Work without Putting Any Order in Them." Nairobi: USK.

Gyimah-Boadi, E. 1994. "Associational Life, Civil Society, and Democratization in Ghana." In *Civil Society and the State in Africa*, ed. John W. Harbeson, Donald Rothchild, and Naomi Chazan. Boulder, Colo.: Lynne Rienner.

Harbeson, John W. 1994. "Civil Society and Political Renaissance in Africa." In *Civil Society and the State in Africa*, ed. John W. Harbeson, Donald Rothchild, and Naomi Chazan. Boulder, Colo.: Lynne Rienner.

Harbeson, John W., Donald Rothchild, and Naomi Chazan, eds. 1994. *Civil Society and the State in Africa.* Boulder, Colo.: Lynne Rienner.

Helmich, Henny. 1990. "New Partnerships in Development Cooperation: NGOs in OECD Member Countries Active in Development Cooperation: Trends of the 1980s and Challenges for the 1990s." In *Directory of Non-Governmental Development Organizations in OECD Member Countries.* Paris: Development Center, OECD.

Hirst, Paul Q., ed. 1989. *The Pluralist Theory of the State: Selected Writings of G. D. H. Cole, J. N. Figgis, and H. J. Laski.* New York: Routledge.

Holmquist, Frank. 1984. "Self-help: The State and Peasant Leverage in Kenya." *Africa* 54(3): 72–91.

Hultman, Tammi. 1992a. "Africans Push More Ambitious Environment Goals." *Africa News* 36, no. 3 (June 8–21): 1–2.

Hultman, Tammi. 1992b. "Profile: I Am a Woman, Wangari Maathai." *Africa News* 36, no. 3 (June 8–21): 3.

Huntington, Samuel. 1968. *Political Order in Changing Societies.* New Haven, Conn.: Yale University Press.

Huntington, Samuel. 1991. "Democracy's Third Wave." *Journal of Democracy* 2(2): 12–34.

Hyden, Goran. 1983. *No Shortcuts to Progress: African Development Management in Perspective.* Berkeley: University of California Press.

Hyden, Goran, and Michael Bratton, eds. 1992. *Governance and Politics in Africa.* Boulder, Colo.: Lynne Rienner.

Inter-Action. 1986. *Diversity in Development: US Voluntary Assistance to Africa.* Washington, D.C.: American Council for Voluntary International Action.

Jackson, Robert H., and Carl G. Rosberg. 1982. *Personal Rule in Black Africa: Prince, Autocrat, Prophet, Tyrant.* Berkeley: University of California Press.

Jackson, Robert H., and Carl G. Rosberg. 1986. "Sovereignty and Underdevelopment: Juridical Statehood in the African Crisis." *Journal of Modern African Studies* 24(1): 1–31.

Jaffer, Murtaza. 1991. "Discussion Notes on the NGO Coordination Act." Paper presented at Institute for Development Studies, University of Nairobi NGO seminar, February 8.

Kahare, Njogu, Nyandarua district advisor. 1993. "General Report on Nyandarua District, 1987–1992." Nairobi: GBM.

Kanyinga, [Henry] Karuti. 1992. "A Changing Development Space? The Local Politics of Development in Kiambu, Kenya, 1982–92." Paper prepared for the Scandinavian Institute of African Studies project "The Social and Political Context of Structural Adjustment Programs in Sub-Saharan Africa."

Kanyinga, [Henry] Karuti. 1993. "The Socio-Political Context of Non-Governmental Organizations (NGOs) in Kenya." Revised version of a paper presented at the Scandinavian Institute of African Studies workshop "The Political and Social Context of Structural Adjustment in Sub-Saharan Africa," Harare, Zimbabwe, March 3–6, 1991.

Karimi, Joseph, and Philip Ochieng. 1980. *The Kenyatta Succession.* Nairobi: Transafrica Book Distributors.

Karobia, Jacinta N. n.d. "Report on Kitui Village (Igloo City)." Nairobi: USK.

Kasfir, Nelson. 1976. *The Shrinking Political Arena: Participation and Ethnicity in African Politics, with a Case Study of Uganda.* Berkeley: University of California Press.

Kenya National Council of Social Services (KNCSS). 1987. "Current List of NGOs in Kenya." Nairobi: KNCSS.

Kenya National Council of Social Services (KNCSS). 1989. "A Preliminary Report of the KNCSS 'Facing the Nineties' Conference." Nairobi, August.

Kenya Times. Nairobi: Kenya Times Media Trust.

Khapoya, Vincent B. 1980. "Kenya under Moi: Continuity or Change." *Africa Today*, no. 1: 17–32.

Kibe, Matthew. n.d. "Our Reflections and Actions: Interviews with (Father) Grol, Fabio (Dallape), and Ezra (Mbogori)." Nairobi: USK.

Kinyanjui, Kabiru. 1989. "The African NGOs in Context." Paper presented at NGOMESA workshop "The African NGO Phenomenon: A Reflection for Action," Gaborone, Botswana, May 15–19.

Kriesi, Hanspeter. 1988. "The Interdependence of Structure and Action: Some Reflections on the State of the Art." In *From Structure to Action: Comparing Social Movement Research Across Cultures*, ed. Bert Klandermans, Hanspeter Kriesi, and Sidney Tarrow. *International Social Movement Research* 1: 349–68.

Leeds, Anthony, and Elizabeth Leeds. 1976. "Accounting for Behavioral Differences: The Political Systems and the Responses of Squatters in Brazil, Peru and Chile." In *The City in Comparative Perspective*, ed. John Walton and Louis Masotti. New York: Wiley.

Leemans, Annelis. 1982. "Urban Community Development: The Approach of Undugu." *Africa Journal of Sociology* 3(1): 13–29.

Lekyo, Christopher, ed. 1989. *Recommendations to the Government of Kenya on Supportive Policy and Legislation for Voluntary, Non-Profit Non-Governmental Organizations' Development and Welfare Activities*. Nairobi: KNCSS.

Maathai, Wangari. [1980]. *The Green Belt Movement*. Nairobi: GBM.

Maathai, Wangari. 1988. *The Green Belt Movement: Sharing the Approach and the Experience*. Nairobi: Environmental Liaison Center International.

Maathai, Wangari. 1991. "People's Rights, Participation and Resources: Decisions and Actions for Sustainable Development with Justice and Equity." Plenary speech at World Women's Congress for a Healthy Planet, Miami, Fla., November 8–12.

Maathai, Wangari. 1992. Interview by South African journalists. November 19.

Maathai, Wangari. 1993. Untitled lecture to participants in Pan-Africa Green Belt Movement seminar, Nairobi, March.

Mbaya, V. 1993. GBM Treasurer Report to Author. Mimeo.

Mbithi, Philip, and Carolyn Barnes. 1975. *A Conceptual Analysis of Approaches to Rural Development*. Nairobi: University of Nairobi Press.

Mbogori, Ezra. 1992. *The Undugu Story*. Nairobi: USK.

Meegan, Michael K. 1992. Letter to NGO Standing Committee. July 14.

Micou, Ann McKinstry, and Birgit Lindsnaes, eds. 1993. *The Role of Voluntary Organizations in Emerging Democracies*. Denmark and New York: Danish Center for Human Rights and Institute of International Education.

Migdal, Joel S. 1988. *Strong Societies and Weak States: State-Society Relations and State Capabilities in the Third World*. Princeton, N.J.: Princeton University Press.

Mitullah, Winnie. 1990. "NGOs: Options for African Governments or Intruders?" Paper presented at the Center for African Studies, University of Edinburgh, October 24.

NANGOF. 1992. *A Guide to the Creation and Sustenance of an Enabling Environment for NGOs in Namibia*. Consultancy report to the Namibia NGO Forum (NANGOF) by Christopher Lekyo.

Ngethe, Njuguna, and Henry Kanyinga. 1990. "Non-Governmental Organizations in Kenya: The Context of the NGOs Coordination Act, 1991." Paper prepared for the workshop on NGOs Coordination Act 1991, Nairobi, February.

Ngethe, Njuguna, Winnie Mitullah, and Mutahi Ngunyi. 1990. "Government-NGO Relationship in the Context of Alternative Development Strategies in Kenya." In *Critical Choices for the NGO Community: African Development in the 1990s*. Proceedings from conference, Center for African Studies, University of Edinburgh, May.

Ngethe, Njuguna, and Kenneth Odero. 1992. "Farmers' Organizations in Kenya: Interest Groups or State Agents?" Draft paper at the Institute for Development Studies, University of Nairobi.

NGOSC. 1991a. "Concerns and Recommendations of NGOs on the Act." Nairobi, February.

NGOSC. 1991b. "Memorandum to Donors in Kenya." April 6.

NGOSC. 1991c. "Minutes of Meeting between Standing Committee of NGO Network and the Office of the President (OOP)." March 15.

NGOSC. 1991d. "Minutes of Meeting between Standing Committee of NGO Network and Representatives of Donor Agencies (DA) in Kenya." March 26.

NGOSC. 1991e. "Report of the Proceedings of the First IDS/NGO Seminar of February 1991." Nairobi.

NGOSC. 1991f. "Report of the Proceedings of the Second National Workshop of the NGO Network, April 1991." Nairobi.

NGOSC. 1991g. "Report of the Proceedings of the Third National Workshop of the NGO Network, October 1991." Nairobi.

NGOSC. 1991h. "Report of the Proceedings of the Fourth National Workshop of the NGO Network, November 1991." Nairobi.

NGOSC. [1992a]. "Internal Memo" [June].

NGOSC. 1992b. "Minutes of Meeting of Standing Committee of NGO Network." July 8.

NGOSC. 1992c. "Notes on the NGO Standing Committee Meeting with the Attorney General." August 18.

NGOSC. 1992d. "Notice to All NGOs." June 15.

NGOSC. 1992e. "The Private Voluntary Organizations Act, 1992."

NGOSC. 1992f. "A Report of the NGO Standing Committee on the NGO Act: Issues and Evolution of the NGO Position." Nairobi, May.

NGOSC. 1992g. "Report of the Proceedings of the Fifth National Workshop of the NGO Network, February 1992." Nairobi.

NGOSC. 1992h. "Report of the Proceedings of the Sixth National Workshop of the NGO Network, July 1992." Nairobi.

NGOSC. 1992i. "Report of the Proceedings of the Seventh National Workshop of the NGO Network, October 1992." Nairobi.

NGO Task Force. 1991. "Towards a New Vision for Non-Governmental Organizations in Development." A Consultation Report to Establish a Regional Reflection and Development Center for NGOs in Eastern and Southern Africa. Nairobi, May.

Ngunyi, Mutahi G., and Kamau Gathiaka. 1993. "State-Civil Institutions' Relations in Kenya in the 1980s." Manuscript available at IDS, University of Nairobi.

Njiru, James, Minister of Culture and Social Services. 1989. Closing speech to NGOs at the Kenya National Council of Social Services seminar, Nairobi, August 18.

O'Donnell, Guillermo, Phillipe Schmitter, and Laurence Whitehead. 1986. *Transitions from Authoritarianism.* 4 vols. Baltimore: Johns Hopkins University Press.

Omoro, Ben. 1986. "Focus on NGOs: What Is the NGO Controversy About." Parts 1–3. *Daily Nation* (Nairobi), October 8–10.

Organization for Economic Cooperation and Development (OECD). 1990. *Directory on Non-Governmental Organizations in OECD Member Countries*. Paris: Development Center, OECD.

Oyugi, Hezekiah, permanent secretary in Office of the President, in charge of provincial administration and internal security. 1986. Speech to NGO conference, Nyeri, Kenya.

Peace Foundation Africa. 1992. *Bureau of Electoral Education, Research and Monitoring (BEERAM)*. Nairobi: BEERAM.

Piven, Frances, and Richard Cloward. 1977. *Poor Peoples Movements: Why They Succeed and How They Fail*. 1st ed. New York: Pantheon Books.

Pratt, D. Riley. 1992. "Slum and Squatter Settlements in Nairobi." In *Readings on Environmental Issues in Kenya: Papers on Environment and Development*, ed. Jack Shepherd. Papers by participants in the Dartmouth College 1992 Kenya Environmental Foreign Study Program, Hanover, N.H.

Quereshi, Moeen. 1988. "The World Bank and NGOs: New Approaches." *The Bank's World* (July): 12–14.

Republic of Kenya. 1966. *Sessional Paper no. 1, 1966*. Nairobi: Government Printer.

Republic of Kenya. 1989. *Five Year Development Plan, 1989–1993*. Nairobi: Government Printer.

Republic of Kenya. 1990a. *Nakuru and Nyandarua Intensified Forestry Extension Project*. Mimeo.

Republic of Kenya. 1990b. *Non-Governmental Organizations Coordination Act, 1990*. Nairobi: Government Printer.

Republic of Kenya. 1991a. Letter to NGO Standing Committee from permanent secretary, Office of the President, in charge of provincial administration and internal security. May 30.

Republic of Kenya. 1991b. *Statute Law (Repeal and Miscellaneous Amendments Act), 1991*. Nairobi: Government Printer.

Republic of Kenya. 1992. *Statute Law (Repeal and Miscellaneous Amendments Act), 1992*. Nairobi: Government Printer.

Republic of Kenya. 1993. *Nakuru and Nyandarua Intensified Forestry Extension Project Draft Work Plan 1993*. Mimeo.

Rothchild, Donald, and Naomi Chazan, eds. 1988. *Precarious Balance: State and Society in Africa*. Boulder, Colo.: Westview.

Salmen, F. Lawrence, and A. Paige Eaves. 1989. *World Bank Work with Non Governmental Organizations*. Working Paper no. 305. Washington, D.C.: World Bank.

"Save our Trees." [1982]. *True Love*. Special Report (November 7): 7–8.

Settlements Information Network Africa (SINA). 1986. "Case Study of Undugu Society Squatter Upgrading in Nairobi." *SINA Newsletter*, Nairobi, December.

Shepherd, Jack, ed. 1992. *Readings on Environmental Issues in Kenya: Papers on Environment and Development*. Papers by participants in the Dartmouth College 1992 Kenya Environmental Studies Foreign Study Program, Hanover, N.H.

Smillie, Ian, and Henny Helmich, eds. 1993. *Non-Governmental Organizations and Governments: Stakeholders for Development.* Paris: Development Center, OECD.

Smith, Brian. 1987. "An Agenda of Future Tasks for International and Indigenous NGOs: Views from the North." *World Development* 15 (autumn suppl.): 87–94.

Society (weekly newsmagazine). 1992–93. Nairobi: Nyamora Publications.

The Standard. Nairobi: Standard Newspapers.

Stepan, Alfred. 1988. *Re-thinking Military Politics: Brazil and the Southern Cone.* Princeton, N.J.: Princeton University Press.

Stremlau, Carolyn. 1987. "NGO Coordinating Bodies in Africa, Asia, and Latin America." *World Development* 15 (autumn suppl.): 213–26.

Swinnerton, R. C. F. 1994. "Japan Raises Its Profile in Africa." *Africa Recovery* 7(3–4): 34–35.

Tandon, Yash. 1991. "Foreign NGOs, Uses and Abuses: An African Perspective." *IFDA Dossier* 81 (April/June): 67–78.

Tarrow, Sidney. 1989. *Struggle, Politics and Reform: Collective Action, Social Movements and Cycles of Protest.* Cornell University, Western Societies Paper no. 21. Ithaca, N.Y.: Cornell University Press.

Tarrow, Sidney. 1991. "'Aiming at a Moving Target': Social Science and the Recent Rebellions in Eastern Europe." *PS: Political Science and Politics* 24 (March): 12–20.

Throup, David. 1987. "The Construction and Destruction of the Kenyatta State." In *The Political Economy of Kenya*, ed. Michael Schatzberg. New York: Praeger.

Tilly, Charles. 1978. *From Mobilization to Revolution.* Englewood Cliffs, N.J.: Prentice-Hall.

Topouzis, Daphne. 1990. "Wangari Maathai: Empowering the Grassroots" (interview). *Africa Report* (November–December): 30–32.

United Nations Children's Fund (UNICEF). 1993. *The State of the World's Children, 1993.* New York: Oxford University Press.

United Nations Development Program (UNDP). 1989. *Development Cooperation Report—Kenya.* Nairobi: United Nations.

USK. 1980. "Is Undugu an Established Institution." Nairobi: USK.

USK. [1983]. "Housing Scheme for Kitui Village." Nairobi: USK.

USK. [1986a]. *Evaluation Report.* Nairobi: USK.

USK. [1986b]. "Kinyago Housing Project." Nairobi: USK.

USK. [1986c]. "Kinyago Low Cost Housing Project." Nairobi: USK.

USK. 1986d. "Planning Paper 1986." Nairobi: USK.

USK. 1986e. "Report on Low Cost Housing Program with Emphasis on Kinyago Village." Compiled by Jennifer Kariuki, Undugu Business Advisory Services. Nairobi: USK.

USK. [1986f]. "Undugu Low Cost Housing Program." Nairobi: USK.

USK. [1988a]. "Community Health Program: Annual Report, 1987."
Nairobi: USK.

USK. [1988b]. "Fifteen Years of Undugu." Nairobi: USK.

USK. 1988c. "Images of Undugu and Friends. Fifteen Years of Undugu."
Nairobi: USK.

USK. 1989. *Annual Report, 1988*. Nairobi: USK.

USK. 1990a. *Annual Report, 1989*. Nairobi: USK.

USK. [1990b]. "Business Development Unit: Annual Report, 1988–89."
Nairobi: USK.

USK. 1992. *Biennial Report, 1990–91: Experience in Community Development.* Nairobi: USK.

USK. n.d.a. "Community Organization Department." Nairobi: USK.

USK. n.d.b. "Export Unit Report." Nairobi: USK.

USK. n.d.c. "Kibera Program Annual Report." Nairobi: USK.

USK. n.d.d. "The Undugu Society Constitution." Nairobi: USK.

USK. n.d.e. "USK: Integrated Approach." Nairobi: USK.

Waruhiu, Rose. 1989. "Development of Mechanism for NGO Coordination and Capacity Building: A Preliminary Report to the Kenya National Council of Social Services." Nairobi, October.

Women's Environment and Development Organization (WEDO). 1994a. "Five Regional Roads to Beijing: Twists, Turns and NGO Action." *WEDO News and Views* 6(1): 11.

Women's Environment and Development Organization (WEDO). 1994b. "NGOs Gaining More Access to UN Deliberations." *WEDO News and Views* 7(2): 3.

Weekly Review. Nairobi: Stellagraphics Publishers.

Widner, Jennifer A. 1992. *The Rise of a Party-State in Kenya: From "Harambee!" to "Nyayo!"* Berkeley: University of California Press.

World Bank. 1982. "Cooperation between the World Bank and Non-Governmental Organizations." Mimeo, July.

World Bank. 1989. *Sub-Saharan Africa: From Crisis to Sustainable Growth*. Washington, D.C.: World Bank.

World Bank. 1990. *How the World Bank Works with Nongovernmental Organizations*. Washington, D.C.: World Bank.

World Bank. 1992. *World Development Report 1992: Development and the Environment*. Washington, D.C.: World Bank.

World Bank. 1994. *Better Health in Africa: Experience and Lessons Learned*. Washington, D.C.: World Bank.

Young, Crawford. 1988. "The Colonial State and Its Political Legacy." In *Precarious Balance: State and Society in Africa*, ed. Donald Rothchild and Naomi Chazan. Boulder, Colo.: Westview.

Index

135

About the Author

STEPHEN N. NDEGWA is assistant professor of government at the College of William and Mary. He received his Ph.D. from Indiana University and was previously a visiting research associate at the University of Nairobi in 1992–93. He has conducted research on NGOs and civil society in Kenya, Zimbabwe, and Namibia and his publications have appeared in the *International Journal of Comparative Sociology* and the *African Studies Review*.

Notes:

Wave facilitate elections of directors, trustees, donors. The Biography/mission statements of each participant is available for review on Wave side. we handle the vote on our system.

University groups: teachers, lawyers, Society, Society